NVQs, Standards and Competence

IMI *information service*

NVQs, Standards and Competence

A Practical Guide for Employers, Managers and Trainers

SECOND EDITION

Shirley Fletcher

KOGAN PAGE

To Dale and Kelly

First published in 1991
Reprinted in 1991, 1992
Second edition 1994

Apart from any fair dealing for the purposes of research or private study, or criticism or review, as permitted under the Copyright, Designs and Patents Act, 1988, this publication may only be reproduced, stored or transmitted, in any form or by any means, with the prior permission in writing of the publishers, or in the case of reprographic reproduction in accordance with the terms of licences issued by the Copyright Licensing Agency. Enquiries concerning reproduction outside those terms should be sent to the publishers at the undermentioned address:

Kogan Page Limited
120 Pentonville Road
London N1 9JN

© Shirley Fletcher, 1991, 1994

British Library Cataloguing in Publication Data

A CIP record for this book is available from the British Library.

ISBN 0 7494 1327 1

Typeset by Saxon Graphics Ltd, Derby
Printed and bound in Great Britain by
Biddles Ltd, Guildford and King's Lynn

Contents

Part III
Help Menu: Information, Addresses and References for Practitioners

Acknowledgements

The author wishes to acknowledge contributions from the following individuals and organisations. Some of them she has worked with closely in the past; others, not currently clients, kindly responded to a request for information.

All the individuals concerned supplied helpful information and gave generously of their time despite a tight schedule. The author would like to record her appreciation for their involvement.

Jackie Hall
  APL Project Director (92)

Management Charter Initiative

DO Nick Collins
  Project Coordinator

London Fire & Civil Defence
Authority

Barrie Oxtoby
Gary Ling

The UK Learning Organisations
Network

Preface

New competence-based standards and National Vocational Qualifications continue to be tested and introduced across all industries. This revised edition aims to provide help to those undertaking their introduction.

For most companies, a detailed understanding of the technicalities of standards development will not be required. However, a brief review of technical details is provided to assist understanding of the key concepts and issues which underlie the new structure of standards and assessment. Readers interested in further technical information will find the reference section of assistance. Those who require guidance on specific questions should turn to the 'Quick Reference Guide' in the Help Menu (p 157).

Part I provides employers and managers with a strategic overview of recent developments in the field of competence-based provision, with specific emphasis on the potential benefits and challenges that these developments present for companies in the UK. Key questions and checklists to aid decision-making are included. Part I will also be of interest to senior training staff and to personnel professionals who need to know more about the purpose, structure and resource implications of implementing recent actions for change.

Part II takes training practitioners, and those with responsibility for 'hands on' implementation of change, step by step through the introduction of NVQs and the various uses of competence-based standards. The final chapters provide a brief overview and general guidance on how to make the best use of new competence-based developments within your company.

Checklists and charts provide user-friendly reference documents.

In this revised edition, new case studies and information sections have been included to outline latest related developments such as Training and Enterprise Councils, Investors in People, Assessor and Verifier Awards, and the 'Common Accord'.

The new 'information sections' also outline such developments as what financial support is available to employers and individuals.

Lists of Lead Bodies and Awarding Bodies have been updated and a full list of Training and Enterprise Councils added.

Part One

The Company Perspective: Understanding and planning

Introduction

- What are NVQs?
- What are standards of occupational competence?
- Why should my company introduce them?
- What are the resource implications?
- How do we get these standards?
- What do we do with them when we have them?
- Why do we have to change from the old system of standards and qualifications?

These are just some of the questions currently being asked by employers, managers and trainers across all industries in the UK. Many more such questions are listed in the Quick Reference Guide on page 157, along with the sections where readers will find the answers. But for many people, perhaps the biggest question is why these changes are taking place at all.

BACKDROP TO DEVELOPMENTS

During the 1980s a clear picture emerged in the UK – reports outlined imminent demographic changes, an unstable employment market, a 'skills gap' and a lack of economic competition with our European neighbours. It became apparent that the UK vocational education and training (VET) system was unable to meet the demand for the skilled workforce that employers needed.

In 1981, the then Manpower Services Commission (MSC) produced its *New Training Initiative: An Agenda for Action* (MSC 1981). The key theme of this document was the clearly identified need for Britain to develop a 'flexible, adaptable workforce to cope with the uncertainties that cloud the future'. It suggested that there were two crucial components to this development:

- a comprehensive training strategy
- standards of a new kind.

The new strategy became the three NTI objectives:

- develop skills training
- equip all young people for work
- widen opportunities for adults.

One of the most important aspects of this overall strategy, however, lies in one simple phrase: 'at the heart of the initiative lie standards of a new kind' (MSC 1981).

The new strategy depended upon these new standards becoming available. However, initially, there was confusion about the concept. Didn't we already have standards? What about British Standards? Did the document mean 'training standards' or 'standards required in the workplace'?

COMPETENCE, STANDARDS AND QUALIFICATIONS

Before long, the idea of a 'new kind of standard' became linked to the term 'competence'. The idea of a 'flexible and adaptable workforce' was superseded by that of a 'competent' one as reports such as *A Challenge to Complacency* (Coopers and Lybrand 1985) and *Competence and Competition* created an impact in the training world.

In 1986, the government published a White Paper, *Working Together, Education and Training* (HMSO 1986) which set out plans for a radical review of the UK education and training system. As the title of the paper suggests, a key focus was greater partnership between the providers and users of both education and training. One of the paper's key objectives was to ensure that 'competence and achievement are recognised and rewarded'. It stated that 'arrangements for standard setting and assessment also need improvement' and proposed that 'the structure of vocational qualifications be reformed'.

A report produced earlier that year, *Review of Vocational Qualifications in England and Wales* (MSC/NEDC 1986), had suggested that the existing system of vocational qualifications lacked a clear, readily understandable pattern of provision while suffering from considerable overlap and gaps in provision. It also suggested that there were many barriers to access to qualifications and inadequate arrangements for progression and/or transfer of credit. Finally, it suggested that assessment methods tended to be biased towards testing of knowledge rather than skill or competence, when what was needed by employers was application of skills and knowledge.

The report suggested that a vocational qualification should be defined as:

> a statement of competence, clearly relevant to work and intended to facilitate entry into, or progression in, employment, further education and training, issued by a recognised body to an individual.

It also suggested that this statement of competence should incorporate assessment of:

- skills to specified standards
- relevant knowledge and understanding
- the ability to use skills and to apply knowledge, and
- understanding the performance of relevant tasks.

The government White Paper took all these recommendations forward and solidly agreed that 'vocational qualifications need to relate more directly and clearly to competence required (and acquired) in work'. The radical reform of vocational qualifications therefore became a priority development area.

WHAT ARE THE BENEFITS?

The basic assumptions on which the new system of standards and qualifications operates are that training and work performance can be improved if people know exactly what is expected of them *within the working role*, and if they can be assessed reliably against those standards. In addition, if the expectations are defined by industry itself as explicit standards, and are agreed across industry, then recruitment, selection and maintenance of high standards across the UK can also be improved.

As many companies have found, the key benefits of the new system include increased flexibility of training, an improvement in the identification of training needs and involvement of all staff at all levels in the overall performance (and therefore profitability) of the company.

This is not to say, of course, that the new system is a cure-all for economic problems at either macro or micro level; nor is it a five-minute wonder in terms of the investment required to implement it.

If your company is considering introducing competence-based standards and NVQs, this introduction must be planned, and staff must be trained in its operation. The case studies provided by companies who have begun this work illustrate the importance of these two aspects of change.

MYTHS AND MISCONCEPTIONS

Two main myths/misconceptions hamper understanding of the new structure of standards and qualifications.

NVQs are not training programmes

Many people perceive the new form of qualifications (NVQs, and SVQs in Scotland) as specified training programmes. The 'unit-based structure' of NVQs/SVQs becomes confused with 'modular training programmes'. The point will be clearly made throughout this book that NVQs are not training programmes. A unit of competence is a unit of *Assessment* – it contains explicit standards of workplace performance. Readers should refer to Chapters 2, 3, 4 and 12 for further clarification.

NVQs are not awarded by the NCVQ

A second misconception is that the National Council for Vocational Qualifications (NCVQ) is the awarding body for this new form of certificate. NCVQ is *not* an awarding body, it is an *accrediting body*. NVQs will be awarded by traditional bodies, such as City and Guilds, RSA, BTEC in England and Wales; SVQs will be awarded by Scotvec in Scotland. In addition, some Industry Lead Bodies have become joint awarding bodies. NCVQ puts its stamp of approval on those qualifications which meet its criteria. Readers should refer to Chapters 2, 3, 4 and 11 for further information.

Of course other misunderstandings also occur. These are dealt with in the relevant sections of this book. The reader will find the Quick Reference Guide (p 157) of help in locating answers to particular questions.

— 1 —

Actions for Change

1.1 NEW STANDARDS

Following publication of the government White Paper *Working Together, Education and Training* (HMSO 1986), action to introduce a new kind of standard and new forms of vocational qualifications was taken. The government directed the Manpower Services Commission (MSC, now the Training, Enterprise and Education Directorate, Employment Department) to:

> put in place dependable arrangements for setting standards of occupational competence across all sectors of industry.

It was agreed that these new standards should be defined *by industry* – a dramatic change from traditional forms of standard-setting – and should address questions such as the following:

- Who are the gatekeepers of standards for occupational performance of your workforce?
- Where are these standards?
- Are they accessible to all staff?
- Are they explicit?
- Do they represent expectations of performance or do they reflect what people need to know?

You might consider what your own answers to these questions would be. Traditionally, standards were embedded in curricula: they represented the *inputs* of training – what people had to learn. Assessment has in the past been biased towards testing of knowledge. Here was a shift to standards, and to associated assessment systems, which were to specify and assess *outputs* – what people had to *achieve*.

It is employers who recruit and employ staff, and it is employers who have expectations of the performance of those staff. It follows that employers and industry representatives should set the standards.

1.2 THE STANDARDS PROGRAMME

In order to achieve this, the MSC contacted all remaining Industrial Training Boards (ITBs) and Non-Statutory Training Organisations (NSTOs) and, through a series of conferences organised by the 'Industry Lead Body' (see below) and new 'Occupational Standards Branches' of MSC's head office, put into action a programme of development.

ITBs and NSTOs, as the bodies with responsibility for training within all sectors of industry, were each asked to supply an action plan to provide the following detail:

■ occupations for which each ITB/NSTO had training responsibility
■ a timescale for the development of standards of occupational competence for each occupation
■ a timescale for the development of new National Vocational Qualifications (NVQs) for each occupation
■ an estimated cost of development.

This information enabled the MSC to prepare an 'occupational map' in an attempt to ensure that all occupations across all sectors of all industries would achieve the development of new standards and NVQs.

Where ITBs and NSTOs did not exist (for example in the care sector), a long process of negotiation with a wide range of sectoral organisations began. Representatives from all areas of sectoral activity were brought together and a new kind of organisation – the Industry Lead Body – was formed.

1.3 INDUSTRY LEAD BODIES

Industry Lead Bodies are still being established across all sectors of industry and commerce. Their key responsibilities are the development of industry-defined standards of occupational competence and approval of a framework of new National Vocational Qualifications.

All new NVQs developed by industry need approval of the Industry Lead Body before they can be submitted to the National Council for Vocational Qualifications (NCVQ) for final approval.

Funding for the development of standards and NVQs was provided in part by government. The MSC contributed up to 50 per cent of development costs and provided project managers from The Occupational Standards Branch. The remaining 50 per cent of costs had to be provided by the industry, usually in the form of staff time, accommodation for meetings and workshops, overheads, and so on.

In 1993, NCVQ began the establishment of Occupational Standards Councils – a further grouping of Lead Bodies. The number of new 'councils' to be established is still not clear.

1.4 THE NATIONAL COUNCIL FOR VOCATIONAL QUALIFICATIONS (NCVQ)

Established in 1986, it was to be responsible for

bringing vocational qualifications in England and Wales into a new national framework to be called the National Vocational Qualification (NVQ). (MSC/NEDC 1981)

Initially the new framework was to consist of four levels, based on the following descriptions of standards of achievement:

Level 1
Occupational competence in performing a range of tasks under supervision.

Level 2
Occupational competence in performing a wider, more demanding range of tasks with limited supervision.

Level 3
Occupational competence required for satisfactory responsible performance in a defined occupation or range of jobs.

Level 4
Competence to design and specify defined tasks, products and processes and to accept responsibility for the work of others.

Expansion to level 4+ was to be discussed and the first developments to be undertaken in this area began in 1989, following long discussion and negotiation with the 250 professional bodies. In 1993, agreement was reached that development would not go beyond level 5. (See also GNVQs, p 178.)

The role of the NCVQ

The government set nine specific tasks for the NCVQ:

■ Identify and bring about the changes necessary to achieve the specification and implementation of standards of occupational competence to meet the needs of the full range of employment, including the needs of the self-employed
■ Design, monitor and adapt as necessary the new NVQ framework
■ Secure the implementation of that framework by accrediting the provision of approved certifying bodies
■ Secure comprehensive provision of vocational qualifications by the certifying bodies
■ Secure arrangements for quality assurance
■ Maintain effective liaison with those bodies having responsibilities for qualifications which give entry to, and progression within and from, the system of vocational qualifications into higher education and the higher levels of professional qualifications
■ Collect, analyse and make available information on vocational qualifications and secure the operation of an effective, comprehensive and dependable database
■ Undertake or arrange to be undertaken research and development where necessary to discharge these functions
■ Promote the interests of vocational education and training, and, in particular, of vocational qualifications and disseminate good practice.

The NCVQ and existing examining and validating bodies

The NCVQ (and Scotvec in Scotland) has a new and unique role. It is not an *examining* body – it does not set standards or assess examination papers centrally. Neither is it a *validating* body – it does not approve centres to operate training or learning programmes which lead to the award of a qualification.

In order to understand the NCVQ's role, it is essential to grasp one key point:

NVQs have nothing whatsoever to do with training or learning programmes.

The key is *assessment of performance*. How people learn, what training programme they undertake or what method of training or learning is employed is, in effect, irrelevant. To achieve an NVQ, an individual must *demonstrate competent performance*.

The NCVQ's role, therefore, is not the same as an existing examining or validating body. Its remit is to develop policy for the vocational qualifications system as a whole, to negotiate to achieve the stated objectives from the system and to accredit qualifications of bodies offering awards within the national qualification framework. The NCVQ, therefore, is an endorsing or accrediting body. It approves qualifications which meet its criteria. These criteria are explained fully in the following chapters.

Scotland

The sole awarding body in Scotland is Scotvec, and they have been involved in all developments in England and Wales. The NCVQ's remit does not extend to Scotland, but new Scottish Vocational Qualifications (SVQs) will operate in conjunction with Industry Lead Bodies in the same way as those south of the border.

Scotland already has an operational credit accumulation plan (see Chapter 2) which was developed as a result of the 16+ Action Plan in the early 1980s. This credit accumulation system operates across the vocational education and training field and, like England and Wales, is being extended into the higher education and professional body arenas.

1.5 IMPLICATIONS FOR EMPLOYERS

The forces and actions for change which have briefly been explored in this chapter present new challenges and benefits for employers. Firstly, employers have been provided with an opportunity to directly influence the establishment of agreed standards of performance across all industries. Through representation on, and consultation with, Industry Lead Bodies, employers have been able to state exactly what they expect their workforce to do in each occupational role.

Second, this direct involvement in standard-setting has required employer investment – the standard-setting process takes considerable time and requires commitment to the overall concepts and objectives of the standards programme.

Third, a focus on performance in the workplace requires new forms of assessment of performance. Performance can be assessed most effectively *in the workplace*. Employers therefore have to consider how such workplace assessment systems will operate.

A fourth issue is that development and implementation of new standards and qualifications require a change in attitude. Employers and their staff become much more involved in the individual development process. Assessment of performance in the workplace provides a solid foundation for training-needs analysis and more effective targeting of training. In the last decade, many reports have demonstrated that Britain is nowhere near the top of the list when it comes to investing in training and development of staff.

If employers are to reap the benefits of new standards which specify performance, which require workplace assessment, which lead to national recognition of competent performance, should they not also be investing more in well-targeted training and development?

Last but by no means least is the issue of cost. These changes require an investment in development and a further investment in implementation. A key issue to be considered by users of new systems of competence-based standards and qualifications is one of return on investment. What are the benefits of these new standards and qualifications? Help with this issue is provided in the following chapters.

—2—

The New Structure

2.1 WHAT IS MEANT BY COMPETENCE?

New occupational standards are based on a concept of competence which emerged through long debate. The theoretical discussions regarding a precise definition are adequately covered in a wide range of technical papers. What is of key interest to employers is the applicability of the concept to the real-life employment arena.

The simplest definition of the new concept of competence is:

the ability to perform activities within an occupation.

However, this says nothing about how well the activities have to be performed! The gradual emergence of a more explicit definition occurred as attempts to define clear and meaningful standards continued:

competence is a wide concept which embodies the ability to transfer skills and knowledge to new situations within the occupational area. It encompasses organisation and planning of work, innovation and coping with non-routine activities. It includes those qualities of personal effectiveness that are required in the workplace to deal with co-workers, managers and customers. (Training Agency 1988/89)

This broad, if lengthy, definition attempts to cover all aspects of 'competent' performance in a realistic working environment.

2.2 WHAT EXACTLY ARE NVQs?

The formal definition of a new National Vocational Qualification is that it is 'a statement of competence' which incorporates specified standards in 'the ability to perform in a range of work-related activities, the skills, knowledge and understanding which underpin such performance in employment' (Training Agency 1988/89).

Each NVQ covers a particular area of work, at a specific level of achievement and fits into the NVQ framework.

The NVQ framework

The initial NVQ framework had four levels; agreement has now been reached that level 5 will be the highest and ultimate classification.

	Areas of work			
1				
2				
3				
4				
5				

Figure 2.1 NVQ framework

The levels indicate competence achieved. Level descriptors are given in Figure 2.2.

'Areas of work' refer to occupations such as engineering, catering, agriculture and so on. Various reports on 'occupational mapping' have been carried out in recent years, the most widely known being TOC (training occupations classification). The NCVQ has reviewed the various classifications and also the information provided by Industry Lead Bodies as part of its 'mapping exercise' for standards development. This review has led to a new categorisation of occupations which now forms the basis of the NCVQ database of standards and qualifications.

Level 1
Competence in the performance of work activities which are in the main routine and predictable or provide a broad foundation, primarily as a basis for progression.

Level 2
Competence in a broader and more demanding range of work activities involving greater individual responsibility and autonomy than at level 1.

Level 3
Competence in skilled areas that involve performance of a broad range of work activities, including many that are complex and non-routine. In some areas, supervisory competence may be a requirement at this level.

Level 4
Competence in the performance of complex, technical, specialised and professional work activities, including those involving design, planning and problem-solving, with a significant degree of personal accountability. In many areas competence in supervision or management will be a requirement at this level.

Figure 2.2 NVQ framework – level descriptors

Source: NCVQ 1988a

What do NVQs look like?

The unit-based structure of NVQs provides a hierarchical model of qualifications with standards forming the foundation stones.

As we have noted, the NVQ itself is a statement of competence which can be achieved through accumulation of 'credit' in the form of units of competence. Each unit is made up of defined standards of competence. The structure of an NVQ can therefore be illustrated as in Figure 2.3.

Progression through the NVQ framework can be seen as an incremental development. Increments will take different forms in different occupational areas. This is because individuals are able to increase their competence in a number of ways:

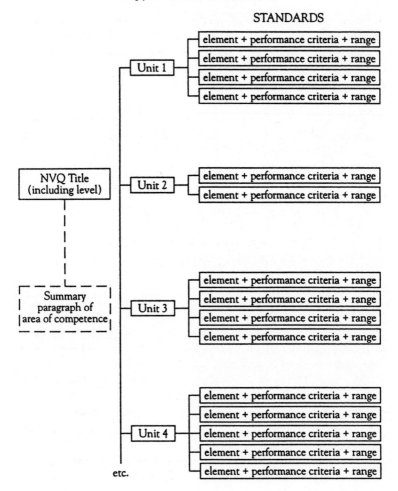

Source: NVCQ 1988a

Figure 2.3 NVQ structure

- By increasing the range of work-related activities they are able to perform
- By mastering more complex work-related activities
- By specialisation.

Individuals may not necessarily progress through the framework in a straightforward vertical order – some lateral progression, across related sectors, is perfectly feasible. For example, there is a great deal of overlap between sectors such as retail and the travel industry. It is quite possible that an individual who has achieved a level 1 qualification in retail, through assessment during work as a retail assistant in a general department store, might progress to a level 2 qualification in travel services through further assessment while in employment within the travel agency department of the same store. This same individual may continue to develop a career in travel services, or may move on in retail management. Either route is possible and qualifications achieved will have relevance in both sectors.

This dual relevance, or 'cross-sectoral applicability', is made possible by a further aspect of the NVQ structure – its *unit basis*, which facilitates credit accumulation.

2.3 NVQs AND TRADITIONAL QUALIFICATIONS

A key aim of the NCVQ's work is that open access to both the acquisition and accreditation of competence should be made available to as many individuals as possible. In addition, the access system must provide flexibility: modes, locations, entry requirements and timescales of learning should not restrict such access.

As noted in Chapter 1, traditional qualifications are tied to a specific course of study and require a set time commitment and set assessment methods, usually involving study at a specified centre. There are also often conditions of entry to study, such as age limits or previously acquired qualifications.

Qualifications are traditionally, therefore, only available if an individual is able to overcome certain barriers or restrictions to access.

2.4 CREDIT ACCUMULATION

Traditional qualification barriers to access include:

- age
- time-based study
- location of study
- specified course of study
- specified assessment methods.

Traditional qualifications are awarded 'en bloc' – individuals obtain the whole qualification or nothing at all. As new NVQs operate on a credit accumulation basis, each qualification is comprised of a number of units of competence, and each unit is independently achievable and separately certificated (see Figure 2.4). Individuals are therefore able to achieve a full qualification by achieving *one unit at a time*. Units can be collected over time, each unit being assessed in the workplace and therefore relating directly to the individual's current work role.

While traditional routes of study (and routes to qualifications) will still be available, and indeed encouraged, the introduction of NVQs means that this traditional mode of accreditation will no longer be the only means available. Widening of access to assessment, removal of time-based study and the introduction of assessment in the workplace have removed restrictions which prevented a wide range of individuals from achieving formal recognition for their skills.

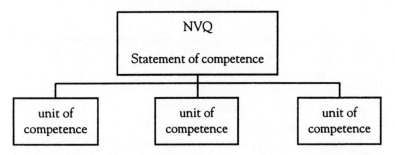

NVQs are not linked to any specified course of study, nor are they time-based; candidates achieve units at their own pace, the primary form of assessment is observation of performance in the workplace and there are no restrictions of age, previous qualifications etc., regarding access to assessment.

Figure 2.4 Unit-based structure

2.5 WHO AWARDS NVQs?

The NCVQ is not an awarding body, it is an accrediting body. It therefore approves qualifications which meet its published criteria (see Part III). The NCVQ covers only England and Wales; in Scotland, Scottish Vocational Qualifications (SVQs) are awarded by Scotvec (the sole awarding body in Scotland) who have agreed to work with the NCVQ to ensure commonality of standards in the UK.

The traditional awarding bodies – City and Guilds, RSA, BTEC, Scotvec, ITD, professional bodies and so on – still award national qualifications. They also submit those qualifications which meet the NCVQ's criteria to the NCVQ for approval as an NVQ.

Awarding bodies have been involved in the development of national standards and have reviewed and restructured their own awards as a result of the changes that have been taking place. As the key to NVQs is assessment, the modes and methods of assessment used by awarding bodies have also been reviewed. Assessment of actual performance in the workplace necessitates change in the role of awarding body assessors and moderators. Credit accumulation requires a change in the structure of national qualifications. Competence-based standards defined by industry have to be used as the basis for all qualifications which are to be submitted to the NCVQ.

UNIT STRUCTURE OF AN NVQ

ABSDA – ASSISTING IN A DENTAL SURGERY

Statement of Competence (NVQ)
Assisting in a Dental Surgery

Units of Competence

1. Control infection in dental surgeries
2. Prepare for and assist during dental treatment
3. Prepare and select instruments/equipment for dental procedures
4. Select, prepare and maintain materials and medicaments for dental procedures
5. Prepare for and assist in general anaesthesia and sedation
6. Assist with dental radiography
7. Assist in dental and medical emergencies
8. Demonstrate oral hygiene to patients
9. Maintain and control stock and equipment
10. Receive and advise expected and unexpected callers
11. Assess, receive and record payments
12. Contribute to the administration of the organisation.

Figure 2.5 Example unit structure

Source: Occupational Standards for Dental Surgery Assistants, NCVQ R&D Report no.1 December 1989.

Some Industry Lead Bodies have decided to work with existing validating and examining bodies to become 'joint awarding bodies'. For example, the Hotel and Catering Training Company is a joint awarding body with City and Guilds and BTEC for NVQs in their industry.

It is important to recognise that the NCVQ itself is *not* an awarding body. It approves qualifications which meet its criteria. (Criteria for approval of NVQs is included in Part III.) Your employees will still, therefore, be certificated by a familiar examining or validating body, but if the particular qualification they achieve has been approved as an NVQ, the certificate will include the NCVQ seal of approval in addition to the awarding body's title.

An example certificate is shown in Figure 2.6.

2.6 WHO DEVELOPS NVQs – AND HOW?

Chapter 1 outlined the government directives which led to the then Manpower Services Commission (now Training, Enterprise and Education Directorate) responsibility for the standards programme and to the establishment of the NCVQ. The same section also briefly reviewed the establishment of Industry Lead Bodies and the arrangements for funding these bodies to undertake development of standards within their industry sectors.

Whilst Industry Lead Bodies (ILBs) have overall responsibility for development of standards and NVQs within their sectors, the actual development must be undertaken *by industry itself*. Each ILB manages a project in which experts from the industry work with a technical consultant to define competence-based standards.

Once the standards are developed, they are circulated throughout the industry, often with a questionnaire, or in test-bed sites to ascertain whether they have real meaning for users and whether they actually reflect workplace practice.

The development of competence-based standards can be a lengthy process, particularly in large, complex sectors of industry where many organisations have interest in 'owning' the development process. Where no established Industry Lead Body exists, one has to be set up. This can involve long negotiations with industry training organisations, employers associations, voluntary bodies, trades unions, professional bodies and so on.

The complexities of the standards development programme are illustrated in Table 2.1 which outlines the stages involved in reaching a final draft of competence-based standards for one sector of industry.

 **City and Guilds** of London Institute

National Vocational Qualification

This Certificate
is awarded to

The holder has one or more formal Records of Achievements
by which this Certificate was earned

Awarded

John A Barnes
Director-General
City and Guilds of London Institute

NCVQ

Director of Training and Development
Hairdressing Training Board

The City and Guilds of London Institute is incorporated by Royal Charter and was founded in 1878

Figure 2.6 An NVQ certificate

Table 2.1 Designing competence-based standards

Action required	
Identify gaps in NVQ framework – which industries do not yet have NVQs?	TEED
Identify/set-up Industry Lead Body (ILB)	TEED
Agree ILB action plan	ILB
ILB completes occupational mapping to identify key work roles within its sector	TEED/ILB
Functional analysis to 'unit of competence' level completed by ILB with help of technical consultant	TEED/ILB
Standards of competence defined for each unit	ILB/TEED
Standards verified by industry through consultation process	ILB/TEED
Refinement of standards based on feedback from industry	ILB/TEED
Units of competence grouped to meet industry requirements (basis of industry's NVQ framework established)	ILB/TEED

In large sectors, the ILB may need to establish its own NVQ framework. This framework would illustrate how the standards had been incorporated into NVQs at various levels (see the NVQ framework on p 26, and would also demonstrate various progression routes.

Once testing of standards is complete, work continues on the development of an associated assessment system and procedures for maintenance of standards (quality control mechanisms).

Involvement of and negotiations with relevant awarding bodies are undertaken to establish quality control and certification procedures and, again, the assessment system is tested within the industry. This process is illustrated in Table 2.2.

When all consultation and negotiation are complete, the entire package of standards, assessment and certification is submitted to the NCVQ by the awarding bodies for approval.

Table 2.2 Designing competence-based assessment

Action *required*	
Determine modes of assessment	ILB/TEED
Develop assessment procedures	ILB/TEED/NVQ
Develop recording procedures	ILB/TEED/NVQ
Test assessment model and procedures in industry	ILB/TEED
Refine assessment model and procedures as necessary	TEED/ILB
Design unit certificate and NVQ certificate	ILB/TEED
Negotiate quality control procedures with awarding body(ies)	ILB/TEED
Determine criteria for approval of assessment centres	ILB/TEED/NCVQ
Determine arrangements for approval of assessors	ILB/TEED/NCVQ

Links with related industry sectors will also be established and transfer of relevant credits (units of competence) between related sectors will be agreed.

The development process involves the use of a functional approach rather than an analysis of tasks or skills. By identifying the key functions, working top-down from sectoral to individual level, a broader view of work activity (and therefore competence) is obtained. This broad view of competence is represented in Figure 2.7.

In this way, the resulting standards do not simply reflect the basic tasks that individuals and organisations undertake, nor do they reflect 'jobs' (many of which can have the same title but differing content or vice versa). An emphasis on *functions* should lead to standards which provide a realistic and explicit definition of *work roles*. Examples of the standards developed in this way are given in the next chapter.

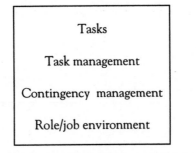

Tasks

Task management

Contingency management

Role/job environment

Figure 2.7 Components of competence (adapted from the Job
Competence Model, Mansfield and Mathews, 1985)

2.7 IMPLICATIONS OF THE NEW STRUCTURE

These radical changes obviously have enormous implications for both
providers and users of vocational qualifications. Changes in the assessment process, the removal of mandatory links to specified training
programmes, the removal of barriers to access and the abolition of
time-based study all lead to increased potential flexibility; they also
require fundamental changes in the approach to training, development and assessment.

For *providers*, these changes mean that methods and modes of training delivery must undergo complete review. Closer liaison between
providers and employers is required. New methods of delivery and a
complete revision of curriculum are needed if the qualification support
system is to operate on a credit-accumulation basis. Arrangements for
continuous assessment and for recording of achievement must also be
put in hand.

For *employers*, the potential is enormous for flexibility of training
and development provision, increased cooperation and involvement
with providers, better targeted training and performance assessment,
improved recruitment, selection, and manpower planning, and ultimately, improved economic performance. (See Fletcher, 1993.)

To achieve this potential, however, employers must be prepared to
invest in the establishment of work-based assessment systems and the
maintenance of quality standards of performance.

Companies are finding that the lead time for introducing competence-based standards and NVQs is longer than the original estimates.
Changing the system requires a complete plan for staff briefing and

training of assessors as well as a possible review of all in-company training.

For *individuals*, guidance has to be provided on the availability and applicability of NVQs and the units of competence of which they are comprised. Once individuals have identified units of competence relevant to their particular needs, further guidance on suitable programmes of development and progression routes will also be required. (See 'TECs', p 112.)

These implications, with their inherent challenges and benefits, are examined in more detail in the following chapters.

—3—

A New Kind of Standard

3.1 A FOUNDATION FOR COMPETENCE

Chapter 1 began with a brief overview of challenges facing the UK and of the new strategy for meeting those challenges which was based on 'standards of a new kind'.

Currently, standards of performance are perhaps the major area of interest to employers. Standards reflect what actually happens in the workplace – and what happens in the workplace affects productivity and profitability. (Qualifications are important to employers for other reasons; we will examine the pros and cons of this issue in the next chapter.)

Also in Chapter 1, you were asked to consider a number of questions relating to the standards currently in use in your own organisation. To refresh your memory, these questions were:

- Who are the gatekeepers of standards for occupational performance of your workforce?
- Where are these standards?
- Are they accessible to all staff?
- Are they explicit?
- Do they represent expectations of performance or do they reflect what people need to know?

For many years, there has been a general concern about Britain's performance in the economic market. This concern is manifest in the enormous interest in the introduction of in-company schemes relating to total quality and the accreditation of companies to meet BS5750 quality assurance.

This emphasis on quality relates directly to the performance of each individual employee.

When recruiting and selecting staff, no doubt you have some form of job and person specification from which to develop a profile of the sort of person you are looking for. For some employers, experience is a key issue; for others, qualifications are high on the priority list.

Many job descriptions and most of the UK vocational qualifications, as well as the education and training system, have not been based on *specification or achievement of precise standards*. As a result, industry has been disappointed in both the quality and actual performance of its recruited employees.

If, as is traditionally the case, standards are based on inputs or what has to be learned, and assessment is biased towards testing of what people know (as in course assignment and examination), it is not surprising to find that actual performance in job roles falls short of expectations and requirements.

However, if standards were based upon expectations of performance, set by industry, and linked to qualifications which could only be achieved through *actual demonstration of the required performance*, then quality of recruitment, selection and actual workplace activity should improve.

The development of nationally agreed standards of competence provides a benchmark for performance across all occupations, provided that industry is fully involved in the development and consultation processes. This was the basic philosophy behind national developments relating to standards (and NVQs). However, from the employers' viewpoint, qualifications are not the main reason for having precise standards. A real test of this 'standard of a new kind' would be its applicability and utility across the spectrum of employment practices.

The issue of utility is addressed later in this chapter. First we need to consider what these new standards offer companies and to review exactly what form they take.

3.2 WHAT MAKES THE NEW STANDARDS DIFFERENT?

Two key aspects of the new competence-based standards make them completely different from those traditionally used in training, vocational assessment and award of certificates. The first relates to the basic concept of *competent performance* and has already been outlined:

competence-based standards reflect expectations of workplace performance;
competence-based standards express **outcomes** *of workplace activity.*

The second key aspect is one which offers considerable potential for future training, development and assessment plans. It is also one which many people fail to grasp – mainly because it requires a complete shift of thinking. Unlike traditional, curriculum-based (input) standards, which are linked to a specific training or learning programme (and also linked to predefined forms of assessment), new competence-based standards are *completely independent* of both training and assessment processes (see Figure 3.1).

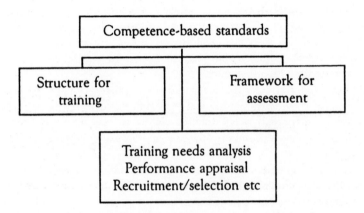

Figure 3.1 Independence of competence-based standards

Because the 'new kind of standard' is focused entirely on required performance (including the application of under-pinning knowledge and understanding), it provides a foundation on which training programmes, and/or assessment processes can be developed.

3.3 WHAT DO THESE DIFFERENCES MEAN FOR MY COMPANY?

Discussions with a range of employers lead to one key answer to this question – *flexibility.*

As the new forms of standards are completely independent of training and/or assessment systems (although they are integral to assessment leading to NVQs), their potential use at organisational level is enormous. The last two sections of this chapter provide some stimulus for thought on this issue.

Organisations which have introduced competence-based standards have recognised the benefits of having explicit statements of performance available to all staff. Some of the benefits include:

- staff know exactly what is expected of them
- assessment to specified standards means training needs can be easily identified
- training can be targeted to real needs
- as standards are not linked to any particular training or learning programme, both in-company and external training can be used as well as a wide range of training methods.

3.4 STANDARDS AND NVQs

New National Vocational Qualifications (NVQs) use nationally agreed standards of competence as the framework for *assessment* of occupational competence.

One of the most difficult concepts for many individuals to grasp was outlined in Chapter 1:

NVQs have nothing whatsoever to do with training or learning programmes

If your company introduces NVQs, therefore, it is not introducing a new training programme, it is introducing a new form of assessment of occupational competence which leads to the award of a National Vocational Qualification. Issues of competence-based assessment are outlined in Chapter 4.

The structure of an NVQ was illustrated in Chapter 2, (see p 28). The foundation stones of all NVQs are competence-based standards, the basic composition of which is

- element of competence
- range statement
- performance criteria.

Elements of competence

An element of competence is a description of something which a person who works in a given occupational area should be able to do. It reflects action, behaviour or outcome which has real meaning in the occupational sector to which it relates. For example:

■ create, maintain and enhance effective working relationships (management competences)
■ inform customers about products and services on request (financial services competences).

The issue of being *outcome-based* is of prime importance. This represents a strong shift away from traditional standards which are based on inputs or curriculum (ie, what has to be learned).

Performance criteria

Performance criteria are statements by which an assessor judges the evidence that an individual can perform the workplace activity specified by the element of competence. In effect, the performance criteria enhance the element of competence by stating explicit measures of outcomes. For instance, the performance criteria in Figure 3.2 refer to qualities of the 'objectives' which are to be set by the individual. The 'objectives' themselves are the *outcome* of this activity.

Performance criteria consist of a short sentence with two components – a critical outcome and an evaluative statement (how the activity has resulted in the required result).

Range statement (and range indicators)

Range statements describe the limits within which performance to the identified standards is expected, if the individual is to be deemed competent.

Range indicators serve the same purpose but some words of caution are relevant. There are two reasons why range indicators rather than range statements may be found in published national standards:

■ Range indicators are often developed as the first attempt at defining more explicit range statements. The presence of 'range indicators' may, therefore, suggest that further development work is being undertaken at national level.
■ In 'generic' occupational areas (such as management or training, which operate across all industrial sectors), it may only be possible to develop range 'indicators'. As these generic standards will be used across a wide range of commercial and industrial sectors, flexibility in specifying the detailed range statement will be a paramount consideration'.

A range statement is a guide to an assessor. A judgement of 'competent' denotes that an individual is able to produce the desired outcomes within the requirements of their work role. This may mean that the individual is able to complete the same activity using a range of equipment or materials, or that they can complete a number of activities within a working context, or within a range of contexts.

If assessment of competence is to be realistic, competent performance in a range of equipment, materials and contexts must be assessed. This is where the range statement serves to 'set the scene' for assessment.

To take our Figure 3.2 example, after the range *indicators* had been examined, and range *statements* specified as appropriate, an assessor would seek evidence of objectives having been set and updated for teams and for individuals, for both short and long term, and using both qualitative and quantitative methods of analysis. In addition, instances of objectives being explained verbally and in writing would be sought as well as examples of single and multiple objective-setting.

When using range statements, an assessor will collect evidence of competent performance across a range of activity. Chapter 4 discusses the new forms of assessment and the importance of collecting evidence of competence.

The example in Figure 3.2 shows how these components might appear in practice. It is taken from a 1990 draft of management competences, developed by the Management Charter Initiative.

Units of competence

When competence-based standards are developed, using the functional approach as described in Chapter 2, the initial analysis provides titles for *units of competence*.

These units of competence represent workplace activity which

- can be undertaken by one individual
- is worthy of separate certification (ie as a 'credit' towards a full NVQ).

Units of competence *are not training modules*. As noted in Chapter 1, NVQs have nothing to do with training or learning programmes. The components of a unit of competence (ie element, performance criteria and range statement) will probably form the structure on which a training programme will be based, but a unit of competence reflects what has to be achieved in the workplace. It is expressed as an *output*

Element II 7.1 Set and update work objectives for teams and individuals

Performance criteria
a. Objectives are clear, accurate, and contain all relevant details including measures of performance.
b. Achievement of the objectives is practicable within the set period given other work commitments.
c. Objectives are explained in sufficient detail and in a manner and at a level and pace appropriate to all the relevant individuals.
d. Objectives are updated regularly with the relevant individuals to take into account individual, team and organisational changes.
e. Individuals are encouraged to seek clarification of any areas of which they are unsure.

Range indicators
Objectives are all operational objectives within the line responsibility of the manager.

Objectives apply to team, individuals and the manager him/herself.

Objectives are: short term
                 long term
                 single
                 multiple.

Setting and updating of objectives involve methods of analysis which are: quantitative
                                                                               qualitative.

Objectives are explained: verbally
                            in writing.

Figure 3.2 Example showing element of competence, range statement and performance criteria (MCI)

of activity. No sequence of learning or learning input is specified – this is an issue for individual employers to determine when deciding on training needs.

Each unit of competence has three components:

- *Unit title*: this refers to the area of competence covered by the unit. A unit title should not refer to a specific *job*.
- *Description of the unit's purpose*: this is not mandatory, but is sometimes added to supplement the title and possibly describe the unit's relationship to other units within the NVQ. For example, a unit on health and safety may be a prerequisite for units involving the use of machinery.
- *Competence-based standards*: elements of competence, range statements and performance criteria form the standards of occupational competence which reflect the expectations of performance.

The example from MCI management in Figure 3.2 demonstrates what these standards look like. The following sections briefly explain the components of standards and relate each component to its use within a business environment.

Further examples of standards can be obtained from Industry Lead Bodies. (See Lead Body list p 179.)

What about knowledge?

This is a question frequently asked about the new competence-based standards – an understandable question when it appears that the focus is totally on performance in the workplace. Those of us who are familiar with assessment processes within traditional qualifications will be aware that there is a 'knowledge bias' within testing procedures.

A common complaint from employers in the past has been that 'qualified people', although recruited on the basis of having achieved a relevant qualification, still need considerable training because 'they know what to do but have little experience of actually doing it'. A valid concern about new forms of standards and qualifications, therefore, is that those who have been able to demonstrate *performance* will 'be able to do, but not understand what they do'!

The issue of the role of knowledge and understanding within competence-based standards was debated long and hard with all partners in the vocational education and training system. The original directive for 'standards of a new kind' and for the 'reform of vocational qualifications' stipulated that it was the 'application of skills and knowledge' that was of importance in competent performance.

Initial ideas implied that knowledge could be identified within competence-based standards as 'elements of competence' or 'performance criteria'. However this proved not to be the case. This approach simply encouraged separate treatment of 'knowledge and understanding', whereas the aim was to provide an integrated expression of competent performance.

Through various exploratory projects it became clear that, in some respects, 'underpinning knowledge and understanding' could be *inferred* from performance (ie the assessor, as a person experienced in the particular occupational field, would be able to make this inference).

A further issue relating to knowledge and understanding concerns the question of transfer of skills – application of knowledge means being able to transfer 'what you know and understand' within different contexts, or to the use of different equipment, or to dealing with contingencies. In this respect, the range statement acts as a guide (for the assessor) to ensure that related knowledge and understanding are assessed.

This section has provided a very brief overview of the technical issues involved in the development of competence-based standards. For those who wish to delve deeper into technical issues, relevant technical documents are listed in the reference section.

3.5 THE USES OF STANDARDS

Consider for a moment how your organisation currently uses standards – if you have them. We have already mentioned that recruitment and selection may utilise some kind of profile for both job and person. What about activities such as manpower planning, performance appraisal, training needs analysis, or judging the effectiveness of training provision?

How about actions for change? Do you refer to standards when considering introducing new technology, or implementing a plan for multiskilling, or restructuring the organisation?

Then there is the question of 'to whom do standards relate?' Do you have standards only for skilled workers (maybe in some form of workshop manual)? Or do you have clear standards for all of your workforce, including management?

The big questions are:

- On what basis do you make decisions regarding the restructuring or reorganisation of your workforce?
- How do you take a 'skills audit' of your workforce?
- What information do you use when making decisions about the recruitment and selection of new staff?
- On what basis are decisions regarding future manpower planning made?
- How do you measure performance?

Perhaps an even bigger question is:

- **how do you define performance?**

We come back to attitudes. Does 'performance' immediately suggest issues at organisational level? Issues of profitability, productivity, competitive advantage in the market place? Or does 'performance' also suggest individual work activity which results in these higher-level measures?

If the latter is true, then you are an employer who has at least considered the importance of the contribution of each member of your workforce to the overall 'performance' of your company. You may well have an appreciation of the key part that explicit, industry-defined standards could play in all employment activities.

Potential uses of explicit standards of performance for all work roles might include:

- identifying training needs within the context of organisational objectives
- designing training programmes
- identifying changes in roles
- planning multiskilling activities
- setting objectives for self-development
- improving performance appraisal systems
- manpower planning.

(See also Fletcher, 1993.)

3.6 CONTEXTUALISING STANDARDS

Nationally agreed standards of occupational competence are, as noted at the beginning of this chapter, a benchmark for competence across a

47

sector. In areas such as management, or training and development, or administrative and clerical work, national standards will be applicable across a wide range of sectors.

At organisation (ie company) level, decisions to 'contextualise' standards may be taken. Some organisations may feel that the national standards need to be enhanced in order to reflect the company mission and objectives. Some may wish to incorporate specific company standards.

There is no reason why this cannot be done. If nationally agreed standards of occupational competence for relevant work roles remain as the basis of any assessment process leading to award of NVQs, then additional information can be added to these standards.

Many organisations may already have invested in development of 'company standards'. Again, these can either be revised to a competence-based format, or incorporated into those agreed by the sector. It is likely that companies will need consultancy support to complete this work. See Case Study on London Fire Brigade, Chapter 6. One area of confusion during the early 1990s has been the introduction of GNVQs. It is essential that GNVQs are not confused with other NVQs when considering company implementation.

—— 4 ——

New Forms of Assessment and Certification

4.1 WHAT IS ASSESSMENT?

This may seem like a very obvious question, but try writing a brief answer for yourself. When you have completed this, try the following questions:

- What do you know/do about assessment of:
  - your company's performance?
  - your department's performance?
  - your section's performance?
  - your unit's performance?
  - individual performance?
  - your own performance?
- How do you assess:
  - training needs?
  - effectiveness of training in your organisation?
- What measures do you use/your company use to assess all of the above?

(See also Fletcher, 1992b.)

Let's try a related area – *certification*. When recruiting staff, do you look for staff with particular qualifications (ie certificates, diplomas etc)? Do you know how individuals are assessed in order to achieve those qualifications? You might also consider what the qualification tells you about the individual?

When you have completed this exercise for yourself, you might like to try the questions on other people within your organisation and compare the answers.

Personal perceptions

The term 'assessment' can be interpreted in many ways. If we talk about 'assessment of the company's performance', then we may be considering measures such as profitability, market share, productivity. Assessment of department or unit performance may lead us to talk about 'qualitative and quantitative measures' and discussions about 'objectives' and 'targets'.

Assessment of individual performance, in a company context, usually refers to systems for 'performance appraisal' – which, sadly, are themselves often an annual ritual rather than an effective measure – or the term may be reminiscent of periods spent at an 'assessment centre' where various tasks, games and discussions led to a form of management profiling.

Quite often, 'assessment of individual performance' is also seen as the domain of occupational psychologists with arms full of psychometric tests and personal files.

A traditional view

Our personal perceptions of assessment are probably shaped by our own experiences of being assessed or assessing. In general, most people's experience of assessment is by formal testing of some kind, whether it be a written examination, verbal report or a form of skills test.

We may all have carried out some form of assessment ourselves, perhaps without even realising it – an interview situation is a prime example of this. Interviewers make an assessment (or judgement) about interviewees based on documentation and discussion, perhaps with a skills test thrown in.

Traditional forms of assessment follow a pattern of formalised assessment – and usually have formalised measures to use in making judgements. For example, let's consider the traditional form of assessment for a vocational qualification:

student registers for and undertakes
specific course of study/training
↓
student completes course assignments
which are assessed by tutors
(written or skills tests)
↓
student takes final examination
or presents dissertation/thesis.

Table 4.1 outlines the measures that are used.

Most traditional assessment methods use a percentage pass mark. Most are also *norm referenced*, ie individual results are compared with the results of others based on a 'normal' or expected pass rate. Figure 4.1 illustrates what this actually means in practice.

While a well-designed learning programme aims to provide all the input (often combined with practical experience) needed to cover a specific vocational area, this traditional form of assessment results in a final grading which represents assessment on perhaps only half of the actual skills, knowledge and understanding which is required.

Many education and training providers have moved forward from this very traditional position and have improved collaboration with employers in order to make learning and assessment more relevant to the actual work role. However, while percentage pass marks remain there will always be questions like 'In which areas was this individual not assessed?' 'Which areas did this individual choose to avoid in the examination?' 'Were any of these areas critical to competent performance?'

Table 4.1 Traditional measures of achievement in vocational qualifications

Assessment method	Measure
Course assignments	50% pass
Final examination/thesis	50% pass

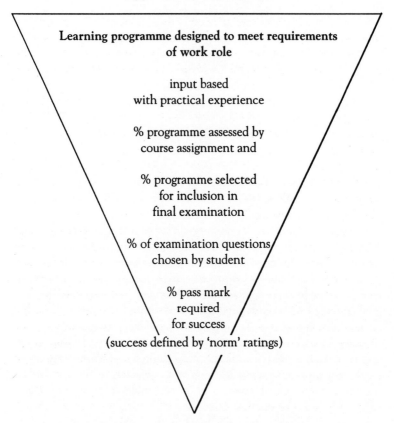

Figure 4.1 Traditional assessment procedures

Competence-based assessment

New forms of assessment (an integral part of NVQs), differ from the traditional approaches in six key areas:

1. a foundation of outcome-based standards
2. individualised assessment
3. competent/not yet competent judgements only (not percentage pass marks)
4. assessment in the workplace
5. no specified time for completion of assessment
6. no specified course of learning/study.

In competence-based assessment, it is *individual performance* which is judged – and judged against explicit standards which reflect not what that individual should know, but the *expected outcomes* of that individual's *competent performance*. How individuals perform in comparison to others is irrelevant.

Only two judgements can be made: either the person has consistently demonstrated workplace performance which meets the specified standards or they are not yet able to do so – 'competent', or 'not yet competent'.

Individuals are assessed in the workplace wherever possible. If assessment is undertaken in connection with the company's implementation of NVQs, individuals will achieve units of competence (and eventually a whole NVQ) at their own pace.

Competence-based standards are available to assessors and assessees. Individuals know exactly what they are aiming to achieve and assessors can provide specific feedback. Assessment on an ongoing basis uses normal workplace performance as its basis, and this continuous assessment process helps in the identification of training needs.

Individuals do not attend a specified course of study (unless the company wish to provide this). Learning can take place on the job, through formal in-company or external courses, through open learning or, indeed, any method which meets both company and individual needs. Training can be targeted to individual needs.

What is being assessed?

Consistency is of prime importance. A one-off demonstration of skill (as in a skills test) is not sufficient for making a judgement about competent performance. As an employer or manager, you need people who can perform in their work role to a *consistently* high standard.

Standards defined in a competence format, as described in Chapter 3, are explicit descriptions of the expected outcomes of workplace activity. When using these standards as a framework for the design of an assessment system, that framework establishes that it is the outcomes of individual performance that will be judged by assessors.

Who assesses?

The primary method of assessment in a competence-based system is *observation of workplace performance*. If assessment uses explicit standards of occupational performance as its foundation, then the logical way to assess whether someone is meeting those standards is to watch them working in that occupation.

The next logical conclusion is, of course, that the best people to assess are workplace supervisors or first-line managers – people who have first-hand and regular contact with the individuals who are being assessed.

For those companies who have identified the benefits of introducing total quality management (TQM) and BS5750,* an assessment system which demands involvement of line managers throughout the organisational structure is perfectly in accord with organisational aims and objectives. One can also argue that this form of assessment simply makes explicit what supervisors and first-line managers should be doing anyway.

However, the implications of introducing competence-based assessment (and NVQs) need careful consideration and planning. Guidance on this planning process is given in Chapter 5.

4.2 HOW IS COMPETENCE-BASED ASSESSMENT CONDUCTED?

We have briefly considered the 'what' and 'who' of both new and traditional competence-based assessment. For most companies who are interested in using new forms of standards and/or qualifications, a prime question is the 'how'.

All assessment is about collecting and judging *evidence*. For the tutor/assessor on a traditional college-based vocational programme, the actual forms of evidence collected are completed course work and assignments and final examination results.

For the workplace assessor, operating within a competence-based assessment system, the actual products of performance provide *evidence* to be matched against specified standards. A workplace assessor will seek evidence of performance which matches the element, performance criteria and range statement for each unit of competence. Where evidence is not available from normal working practice, or would be difficult to generate, the assessor may need to set up supplementary assessments.

---

* Companies which have been accredited with BS5750 have undergone an audit of their quality policy, systems and control. BS5750 includes quality systems, standards and guidelines that complement relevant product or service technical specifications.

For example, a competent worker may be one who is able to deal with a number of contingencies – machine breakdown, sudden changes in workload or priorities, or even a fire. It would obviously not be practicable for an assessor to cause a deliberate breakdown of machinery (or indeed set fire to the building), simply to assess an individual's ability to cope. In this context, therefore, an assessor needs to be skilled in providing opportunities for supplementary assessment. This may involve a skills test, questioning of the individual, or allocating a new task or job.

A workplace assessor requires training in the use of competence-based standards, and in the application of various assessment methods. It is the workplace assessor who 'signs off' an individual as competent, and he/she needs to be confident in this role. National standards and unit awards are now available for assessors – see page 139.

What about quality control?

Any system of standards will only be as good as the quality control mechanism that ensures they are maintained. Within competence-based assessment systems, and particularly within those that lead to award of NVQs, quality control is a prerequisite to operational approval. For NVQs, various systems are in place, but all follow a basic pattern in which the workplace assessors are supported and monitored by *internal and external verifiers*.

In terms of external quality control the awarding bodies have overall responsibility for assessment within NVQs; they award units and full qualifications. External verifiers support and monitor workplace assessors.

Internal quality control is the concern of internal verifiers – in-company 'countersigning officers' – and workplace assessors like supervisors and first-line managers. In 1993, NCVQ and the Awarding Bodies published a Common Accord (see p 171) which aimed to provide consistency in quality assurance across all NVQs.

4.3 NEW FORMS OF CERTIFICATION

What do certificates tell us?

We have already reviewed the traditional pattern of formalised assessment leading to the award of a certificate, diploma, or other form of vocational qualification. At the beginning of this chapter, you were asked to consider a number of questions, one of them being 'What does a qualification tell you about an individual?'

Traditional qualifications usually tell us that the qualification holder has passed the formal assessment process. They may also indicate that the individual has achieved a pass, credit or distinction. This, of course, relates to the percentage pass mark achieved, which, as we noted earlier, is norm-referenced.

NVQ certificates

Let's consider another question: 'What would a new NVQ tell you about an individual?'

A qualification with the NCVQ logo will tell us that the qualification holder has passed the assessment process. It will not include a pass, credit or distinction grading because for NVQs these grades do not exist. It will also tell us that the assessment process involved assessment of actual performance in the workplace as the primary form of assessment. The certificate will also show the *units of competence* which the certificate holder has achieved.

Now consider an interview scenario. A candidate for an interview presents you with copies of 'credits towards an NVQ'. What does this tell you about the candidate?

Under the new national 'credit accumulation scheme', individuals will accumulate credits towards a full NVQ, each credit being a unit of competence. Awarding bodies will provide certificates on a unit level which can be 'exchanged' for a full NVQ once the relevant total of units has been achieved. These units may be stored in what is called an NROVA.

4.4 NATIONAL RECORD OF VOCATIONAL ACHIEVEMENT (NROVA)

The National Record of Vocational Achievement (NROVA) is available to all candidates for assessment leading ultimately to NVQs. All major awarding bodies participate in the operation of the NROVA scheme which is

a common system for recording unit-credits towards qualifications of different education and awarding bodies, in different education and training programmes, in different locations, over varying periods. (NCVQ 1988a)

Roughly translated, this means that an individual can, in his or her own time, collect credits towards an NVQ from a wide range of experience. When he or she has the right collection of credits, they can be exchanged for a full qualification from at least one awarding body.

The NROVA has two main parts:

■ Part 1 provides space for an individual action plan (ie the units that the individual is aiming to achieve and a record of progress)
■ Part 2 contains the certificates and credit notes issued by various awarding bodies.

Part 2 of the NROVA is divided into three sections (see Figure 4.2):
■ the first section will contain certificates or credit notes for units of a qualification which already has NCVQ approval
■ the second section will contain certificates which have been issued for qualifications which do not (yet) have NCVQ approval
■ the third section will contain certificates issued within certain national training programmes such as training credits, usually in areas where there are currently no national qualifications available.

As NVQs are still under development in many areas of industry and commerce, the qualification arena is in a state of transition. Some newly developed or revised qualifications have already been approved by NCVQ, others are awaiting results of industry standards development projects, and some are not recognised by an awarding body at all.

4.5 BENEFITS OF A CREDIT ACCUMULATION SYSTEM (THE NATIONAL RECORD OF VOCATIONAL ACHIEVEMENT)*

■ Easier access to qualifications
■ Units can be built up over time
■ Trainees are motivated by immediate recognition of their achievements
■ Units from different awarding bodies can be brought together in one place
■ Integration of different parts of a learning programme and different modes of learning

* Source: NCVQ 1988a.

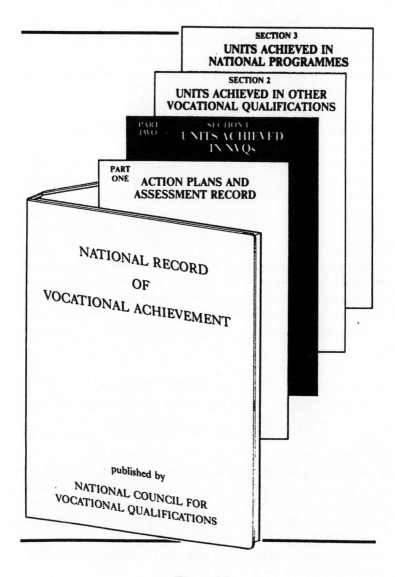

Figure 4.2

- Tutors and trainers will be able to operate within a common system
- More flexible learning programmes can be designed
- A clear statement of the holder's competence is provided in language familiar to employers
- It can record credits from one learning programme to another, throughout life
- Acceleration of progress towards a competence-based national system of qualifications.

4.6 CONDITIONAL ACCREDITATION

One further point to note in relation to NVQs is the issue of *conditional accreditation*. When the NCVQ gives full approval to a qualification, this approval is for a period of five years. Initially however, when the NCVQ felt that the qualification did not yet merit full approval, it awarded conditional status, usually for a period of two to three years.

In practice, this meant that the qualification did not yet meet all the criteria set by the National Council, who expected that this would be corrected at the end of the conditional approval period.

From an employer's point of view, however, it was difficult to know which qualifications had full, and which had conditional, approval. It was even more difficult to find out what the conditions were! Conditional approval arrangements have now ceased.

The NCVQ does publish a booklet called the *NVQ Monitor* which lists all approved NVQs by area of competence. It also provides a list of awarding bodies.

Specific information on individual NVQs can be obtained from the NCVQ database. This includes a description of the qualification, who it is for, its level within the NVQ framework, its component parts and what is required in order to obtain it. The database also allows access to individual units of competence so that standards can be examined to find those particularly relevant to specified areas of employment. Information on conditional approval is not included.

For readers who want to know more about this database, details are provided in the reference section.

4.7 ACCREDITATION OF PRIOR LEARNING (APL)

The accreditation of prior learning (APL) permits the award of credit towards a qualification on the basis of evidence drawn from an individual's past achievements (City and Guilds 1990)

The accreditation of prior learning (APL) is an integral part of assessment for NVQs. It is a process in which evidence of an individual's past achievements within a relevant occupational role can be judged against the standards specified within the appropriate vocational qualification.

Evidence from past achievements must satisfy the requirements of the specified qualification, but can take many forms. Direct evidence of achievement includes 'products' of performance – ie actual outcomes of the individual's work activity. Indirect evidence includes information 'about the individual', such as performance reports, letters from satisfied customers and the like.

The process for assessment of evidence of past achievement differs from any other competence-based assessment only in the preparatory stages. Individual candidates must take responsibility for collecting together evidence which is valid and authentic and matches the specified standards. Initial guidance from a trained adviser will be needed at this stage.

APL and 'skills audit'

The importance of APL at national level relates to the overall objective of widening access to assessment for vocational qualifications, especially among adults who have a wealth of skill and experience and do not necessarily wish to undertake lengthy periods of study.

The credit accumulation system now being introduced makes the APL approach particularly attractive to a wide audience. If 'credit' for existing competence is available, then education, training and development need be targeted only to remedy gaps in occupational competence.

At company level, this last point is probably of most interest. Better targeted training means less 'downtime', and a higher return on investment in training.

A company's workforce can be awarded credit towards nationally recognised qualifications, without having to attend any form of training or learning programme, purely on the basis of evidence of what they can actually do now. This itself is often a motivational aspect for the introduction of both standards and NVQs, providing benefits for both employer and employees. (Guidance on the introduction of APL is provided in Part II: The Practitioner's Perspective).

APL is now being used as a 'skills audit' process within companies. Between 1987 and 1990 a number of early national projects explored the feasibility of operating APL in conjunction with introduction of NVQs. The Management Charter Initiative is now completing its development project which explores the use of APL with experienced managers. Materials to assist companies with implementation of this assessment process have been available since 1991.

The final chapter in Part I draws together the concepts, issues, benefits and implications of competence-based standards, assessment and NVQs and provides a checklist of questions you may wish to ask when considering the introduction of standards and/or NVQs within your own organisation.

—— 5 ——

Key Questions for Decision-making

This chapter provides guidance and stimulus for thought for employers, managers and trainers who are considering the introduction of competence-based standards and NVQs. It assumes that readers are familiar with the key concepts and operational requirements of these new trends in assessment and certification.

To aid you in the decision-making process, key questions relating to the introduction of competence-based standards and new NVQs are provided in a hierarchical order. These questions are:

- Should we introduce standards and NVQs?
- How do we start?
- What needs to be done?
- How we will use standards throughout the company?

There are no model answers; each company will need to make its decisions based on:

- management understanding of the new structure of standards and NVQs
- the perceived benefits of implementation
- consideration of the key issues involved, including resource and cost implications.

The first of these requirements for decision-making can be achieved by reference to Chapters 1–4 of this book. Readers may wish to refer back to appropriate sections for clarification of specific points.

Guidance on the remaining two is included in the following text. Further information on operational issues is provided in Part II, with relevant information sources in Part III. Readers may also find the case studies of organisations currently involved in the introduction process to be a useful reference source.

5.1 DOES MY COMPANY NEED COMPETENCE-BASED STANDARDS AND NVQS?

Potential benefits – competence-based standards.

- Staff will know exactly what is expected of them in terms of outcomes of performance
- Assessment systems (including performance appraisal) can be used effectively to identify training needs
- Training delivery can be targeted to real needs, thus reducing downtime and increasing return of investment in training
- Standards are not linked to any one training/learning programme, so in-company and/or external training can be designed/provided on a completely flexible basis
- Standards will be accessible by all staff, so continuous assessment can be conducted
- Supervisors and line managers can all become involved in ongoing workplace assessment
- Training programmes can be designed, using the standards as the basic design structure, thus making programmes relevant to work roles and more focused on learning which can be put into practice in the workplace
- Standards in competence-based format provide an objective way of looking at current and future manpower needs
- Standards can be used as a basis for recruitment specifications and structuring of interview questions
- Standards would provide consistency and quality and would contribute to the implementation and achievement of BS5750 (see p 54) and/or the introduction of total quality management (TQM).

Potential Benefits – NVQs

- External recognition for employees
- Workplace assessment by in-company staff – all supervisors and

first-line managers involved in day-to-day assessment of performance
- Meets requirements for operation of training credits and other government programmes in providing access to NVQs
- Company assessment and career planning can be linked to progressive structure of national qualifications
- Employees can achieve qualifications without having to attend lengthy periods of study
- Workplace assessment contributes to more effective identification of training needs
- Flexibility of training provision – the company can design its own training programmes, or use external providers who can provide training which is based on the specified standards
- Assessment of evidence of prior achievements can provide employees with credit towards a qualification and therefore recognition for their existing competence
- More effective links with training and education providers can be made with external provision being matched to both company and individual needs.

General guidance

The issue of standards of performance has been the basis of considerable debate and development in the last decade. Many companies have undertaken work to develop their own standards. When considering whether to introduce national standards, a key point to keep in mind is that national standards of occupational competence provide a *benchmark across the sector*.

Using national standards within the company provides a basis for *consistency*, not just within your own organisation, but in other organisations across the sector. There is no reason why you should not 'enhance' national standards to incorporate your own company standards, but if you want to provide access to NVQs for your employees, you must ensure that the core of nationally agreed standards remains intact.

Once the system of NVQs has been operational for some time, it is expected that recruitment will be facilitated. Units of competence and NVQs will provide the currency by which employers will be able to identify what potential employees can do and in which areas they will need further development.

The issue of increased flexibility was outlined earlier (see pp 36, 40 and 59). This is perhaps one of the key benefits for employers who can use competence-based standards as a foundation for cost-effective training needs analysis and total flexibility in delivery of training.

Strategic issues – should we introduce standards and NVQs?

- In what ways do we perceive that the introduction of competence-based standards would contribute to improvement of company performance?
- Are we introducing BS5750 and/or TQM? How would introducing competence-based standards fit in with these plans?
- How would these changes affect job roles and responsibilities?
- Would the introduction of NVQs conflict with any existing company qualification or incentive scheme?
- Do we already have company standards? If so, how will these integrate with national competence-based standards for relevant occupations?
- Which issues need to be discussed fully with trades unions?
- What initial costs (ie registration fees etc) are payable to Lead Industry Bodies and/or awarding bodies?
- What other costs are involved?

Strategic issues – general guidance

Improvement of company performance
This issue must be decided on an in-company basis. A clear understanding of the new structure of standards and NVQs, and of their potential use within an organisation, is essential if informed decisions are to be made.

BS5750 and TQM
It is likely that competence-based standards will provide a complementary approach to the introduction of quality systems. New standards focus on outcomes of performance and on improving quality of individual contributions to company success.

Job roles
If explicit, accessible standards are to be introduced, one assumes they will be used to assess performance and not just to inform individuals of

65

what their performance should be! This has implications for job roles. Who assesses? What extra responsibility/workload is this likely to create? (It should be minimal if a quality recording system is used. Standards should make explicit what line managers and supervisors are doing on a daily basis.)

Existing company qualifications/incentive schemes
If your company already operates an in-company certificate scheme, and particularly if this is linked to some form of incentive or bonus scheme, then you will need to consider how the introduction of NVQs fits in with these arrangements. Even if you are not currently operating such schemes, the issue of incentive/reward needs consideration – people's expectations may well link achievement of qualifications to promotion or other rewards.

Existing company standards
Your existing standards may be in a competence format or in some form of 'profile'. It is important to be clear about any differences between your existing standards and those which form the basis of NVQs (ie national competence-based standards). There is no reason why you cannot enhance or 'contextualise' national standards to meet organisational needs, but if you wish to retain the link with award of NVQs, the core of national standards must remain. In addition, simply adding on standards in another format may directly affect the assessment scheme. It is likely, therefore, that you will need some help in integrating company and national standards – or indeed 'contextualising' national standards for company use.

Trades unions
National standards have been developed by industry. Trades unions are usually fully represented on the development projects. However, some issues may arise which can be dealt with by careful planning. For example, the question of assessors (first-line managers) being responsible for 'signing off' individuals as competent can be the cause of concern in some areas – particularly in those occupations where health and safety are priorities. Similarly, any changes in job roles may need full discussion with relevant trades unions.

Initial costs
For some NVQs, the awarding bodies (sometimes Lead Industry

Bodies as joint awarding bodies), charge an initial registration fee for 'centres' operating NVQs. (A centre can be a company or regions of a company for example.) Other implementation costs will include staff time for briefing/training and any development undertaken. The initial registration fee usually includes costs of materials (copies of standards, recording documents etc).

Other costs
Other ongoing costs may include an annual registration fee (not all NVQs have this) and certification fees. Two forms of certification fee can be payable – one for a unit certificate and the other for a full NVQ. Unit certification costs vary, but average about £6 per certificate (per person). Full NVQ charges include one payable directly to the NCVQ and can be between £30–£125 per certificate. If you introduce the use of the NROVA in company, these can be purchased from the NCVQ (cost currently being revised). You will need one for each person registered for assessment for an NVQ. Assistance with costs funding to help with the implementation of NVQs is available from Training and Enterprise Councils (TECs) – see p 214.

Development and implementation costs – general
In Part II, 'The Practitioner's Perspective' briefly explores issues of whether to wait for national standards to become available or to develop competence-based standards (see Chapter 6). This choice of action has obvious implications for cost. The chart in Figure 5.1 is taken from the Training Agency's *Competence and Assessment* (Training Agency 1988/90) publication and illustrates the key points to consider for development, start-up and implementation of standards.

Initial planning – how do we start?

■ Do we introduce the use of standards in association with NVQs? If not, how will we assess in-company?
■ What are the implications of first-line managers becoming assessors?
   – What training will they need?
   – What about legal responsibility for signing off an employee as competent (ie health/safety)?
   – What support will they need?
■ What are the key occupational roles in our organisation?

■ In which occupational areas would individuals and the company both benefit most from the introduction of NVQs?

■ Who are the Industry Lead Bodies in the appropriate occupational areas?

■ Are national standards available for these occupational roles? (See Part III)

■ Are NVQs available in all occupational areas relevant to our needs?

■ How relevant are national standards to our work roles?

■ Do we want to contextualise the national standards to incorporate our company's objectives or company-specific standards?

■ Who awards the NVQs in these areas? Do we have any existing arrangements with those awarding bodies?

■ How would we motivate staff to operate to the specified standards?

■ Should we consider a phased introduction? Which occupational areas would offer the best test-bed site for a cost-effective implementation?

■ In which occupational area would we introduce standards first?

■ How will we ensure maintenance of standards?

Initial planning – general guidance

Can we introduce standards without introducing NVQs?

Standards have many uses within an organisation, but are of key importance in improving company performance. This can only be achieved if the standards are used within a quality assessment scheme. Providing access to national vocational qualifications may well be a motivational factor for employees and also provides a quality assessment scheme. There is no reason why a company cannot develop its own assessment scheme (particularly if the company is contextualising standards), *and* negotiate approval by an awarding body. This is a viable alternative, but you will need help.

First-line managers as assessors

The extension of line managers' roles may have implications which need discussion with trades unions. (See 'Job roles' and 'Trades unions' in the previous section on strategic issues.) Assessors will certainly need training in the use of competence-based standards and assessment. Support systems will also need to be considered, both for the benefit of assessors and for maintenance of standards.

[A] COSTS IN DEVELOPMENT

- **costs to the organisation co-ordinating development:**
  (normally an Industry Lead Body)
  * personnel – within the organisation at senior, intermediate, clerical, and secretarial grades, and at technical staff grades
  * staff travel – to participate in meetings, etc
  * internal copying, etc
  * meetings – travel and subsistence of participants catering (whether external or internal) accommodation charges
  * consultants fees – to assist in the proper application of the development strategy
  * printing – to present drafts etc for consultation
  * postage/telephone – for communicating with other participants in the development
  * computer development – any costs associated with developing programmes to record results of analysis
  * computer processing – processing data from development
- **costs to organisations providing 'technical' expertise to the development (normally industry, individual practitioners, ILEA's)**
  * Personnel – within the organisation at senior, intermediate, clerical and secretarial grades and at technical staff grades
  * internal copying, etc
  * postage/telephone – for communicating with other participants in the development
- **costs to awarding/accrediting bodies**
  * personnel – within the organisation at senior, intermediate, clerical and secretarial grades and at technical staff grades
  * internal copying, etc
  * postage/telephone – for communicating with other participants in the development
- **costs to industry**
  * personnel – within the organisation at senior, intermediate, clerical and secretarial grades and at technical staff grades
  * internal copying, etc
  * postage/telephone – for communicating with other participants in the development

[B] COSTS IN START-UP

* Same ranges and heads of costs to [A], and in addition to costs under A
* NCVQ – accreditation of award in principle (so, same range of cost heads as for others apply)
* **industry, LIB** – training of participants in implementing the system (NOT Training the individuals who will be assessed under the system)
* **awarding bodies** – participation in training of participants, associated administrative and clerical costs

[C] COSTS IN IMPLEMENTATION

* Same ranges and heads of costs in [A] and [B], and in addition to costs under A & B
* Industry people time dedicated to any stage or level with assessment
  - recording with review of candidate performance
  - coping with errors of competence attribution or mis-attribution

Figure 5.1 *Assessing costs: a) development of standards b) start-up costs c) implementation*

Key occupational roles
You will need to complete an 'occupational mapping exercise'. Remember, standards and NVQs are to be available across all occupations of all sectors of all industries.

Priority areas
You will need to consider the benefits to both individuals and company based on current operational requirements and plans.

Lead Bodies
Part III of this book provides a listing of ILBs and contacts by occupational area.

Availability of standards
ILBs will be able to provide this information. The Training Agency (Qualifications and Standards Branch, Moorfoot, Sheffield) also has a database of currently available and soon-to-be available standards.

Availability of NVQs
The NCVQ publishes a bi-monthly bulletin of new NVQs and all information is stored on the NCVQ database.

Relevance of national standards
You will need to obtain copies of published standards in order to make this decision. Again, ILBs or the NCVQ database will provide this information.

Contextualising standards
If you feel that national standards are not entirely relevant, or that your company standards need to be added to this national benchmark, there is no reason why this cannot be done. However, if you wish to maintain access to NVQs the national standards must remain as the core of assessment. You may need help to do this.

Funding
Check with your local Training and Enterprise Council (see p 214) regarding possible financial support for implementation of NVQs.

Awarding bodies
As explained in Chapter 1, our traditional perceptions of an awarding

body, such as City and Guilds or BTEC, need to change. Where once the syllabus and examination leading to an award (ie a qualification) were their responsibility, they nowadays incorporate standards set by industry into a qualification framework set by the NCVQ. They have overall responsibility for the quality of assessment, but not for assessment methods.

In addition, some Industry Lead Bodies (see Chapter 2) are now also partners in the award structure and have taken on the newly defined awarding body role. NVQs may therefore be awarded by one of the familiar national bodies, or jointly with an Industry Lead Body.

Motivating staff
You will need to identify the key benefits for each group of staff and consider how you will sell the idea of standards and NVQs. Communication networks need careful consideration.

Phased introduction
It is probably best to identify priority areas for introduction of standards and NVQs – perhaps admin and clerical staff, or managers, first, or a key technical area. A clear plan to cover the workforce is essential.

Maintenance of standards
Qualifications submitted to the NCVQ for approval will have an associated assessment model and quality control mechanism. The awarding bodies have overall responsibility for assessment and quality (as it is they who award the qualification). An awarding body moderator (external verifier) will visit the company on a regular basis (or a sample of companies) to check that the assessment system is operating as it should. You should also consider providing in-company support in the form of counter-signing officers (who monitor the work of a number of assessors and countersign completed units of competence). You might also consider regular meetings for assessors to enable them to exchange information and ideas in a peer group environment. This could be combined with, for instance, work on quality circles, or regular departmental meetings.

Operational issues – what needs to be done?

■ Who will be responsible for checking the relevance of standards to our operations?

- Who will undertake contextualisation of national standards if we feel this to be necessary?
- Who takes responsibility for the planning of introduction of standards
  - across the company?
  - in occupational sectors?
  - in departments?
- Who will be the assessors?
- Who needs to be trained?
- Who trains staff to understand and use standards?
- What lead time should we allow for introduction of standards?
- What lead time do we need to allow for
  - briefing of all staff?
  - training of assessors?
- How much of this time would be allocated to
  - development?
  - training?
  - piloting?
- Who will be responsible for the design of training programmes which incorporate national standards? Do they need training?

Operational issues – general guidance

Checking relevance of standards

You will need to ensure that whoever undertakes this task has a clear understanding of competence-based standards and their use and is also well versed in the occupational area. You might consider workshops of relevant staff led by someone (internal or external) who has relevant competence-based experience.

Completing contextualisation

As noted in previous sections, it is probable that you will require external help with this work, unless you have an expert in-house. It is important to ensure that the format of 'enhanced standards' does not detract from the quality of the associated assessment scheme.

Planning introduction of standards

Responsibility for the planned introduction of standards must be allocated to someone who understands what must be done, has the expertise required and is allocated adequate time to control and monitor the process. A hierarchical structure might be adopted with each division or department having a responsible officer who reports to a senior manager.

Deciding on assessors

This is a key decision. Assessors must have sufficient contact with candidates to be able to make a fair and confident judgement of competent performance. They must also, wherever possible, be willing to undertake the role – reluctant assessors will not undertake quality assessment.

Who needs to be trained?

Anyone who will be using the standards for assessment purposes will need to be trained in the principles and concepts of competence-based assessment, and the use of occupational standards. They will also need to understand the procedures associated with the assessment system. If trainers are to be involved in redesign of training programmes, they will need training in competence-based design. A general briefing and information-providing session for the company as a whole would also be a good idea!

Who trains staff to understand and use standards?

As with all training, you have the choice. Some ILBs provide training, some external training providers have expertise in this area. Be clear about the purpose of training: is it briefing on competence-based standards generally, or occupationally-specific training you need?

Lead time

This will depend on how many occupational areas are involved in your implementation plan and whether you are planning a phased introduction. Most companies find that the lead time to actual operation of NVQs is longer than their original estimates. Again, this varies if you are contextualising standards.

Design of training programmes

If you plan to redesign your in-company training programmes, then your own trainers will need training in competence-based design. If you use external providers, make sure they can design training to the competence-based standards you are using.

Further development – how will we use the standards throughout the company?

- Do we have a performance appraisal system? Would we want to redesign this to incorporate national standards?
- Do we have a training policy?
- Do we have a strategic training plan?
- Is our current training plan based on a standards approach?
- Is our current recruitment/manpower planning strategy based on a standards approach?

Further development – general guidance

Performance Appraisal

As you are considering the introduction of in-company assessment leading to NVQs, it makes sense to consider how this links with any existing, or planned, performance appraisal system. This will require a review of the current system and an examination of how competence-based standards of performance can be incorporated into current procedures. You might consider whether formative assessment (ie over time, on a continuous basis) will contribute to the summative assessment (annual performance appraisal and report).

Training policy and strategic plan

If you have a current training policy and strategic plan, this will need review based on redesigned training programmes and procedures which will accompany the introduction of NVQs. With a competence-based system, you will have more flexibility in training delivery: training needs can be identified on an ongoing basis, as part of normal assessment procedures. How will you make best use of this flexibility in your annual training plans?

Recruitment and manpower planning

You may want to consider how you can use the standards to redraft recruitment specifications and to facilitate forecasting of future manpower needs. The units of competence will give you a clear idea of the functions carried out in your organisation; this information can also assist with plans for multiskilling or for the introduction of new plant and technology.

5.2 NVQS AND TRAINING PROGRAMMES

At the risk of labouring a point, it is probably still worth reminding you that NVQs are concerned with *assessment of workplace performance* and not with training programmes.

Many companies, even those who are beginning to introduce NVQs, still ask how they can get their training programmes accredited by the NCVQ. The short answer is *you can't!*

However, if your in-company training programmes are revised so that they are based on nationally agreed standards of competence, they can, when combined with competence-based assessment, provide *evidence* of competence.

No doubt this sounds very confusing. This dilemma is indicative of the difficulty in switching their thinking to accommodate the new nature of qualifications. You need to keep in mind that NVQs are not training programmes – units of competence are not units (or modules) of training, but units of *assessment*. If your training programmes include assessment of competence (ie performance), then this assessment is providing evidence of competence. You will recall that competence-based assessment requires *sufficient* evidence of competence performance – sufficient for a confident judgement to be made. This evidence will come from many sources, including performance assessed in the course of training programmes.

In Chapter 4, we reviewed the traditional form of qualification. Under traditional rules, training which is undertaken in-company can be reviewed and awarded a 'credit rating' towards a qualification. This system of credit rating does not apply to NVQs.

Individuals do not achieve NVQs by simply completing training or learning programmes, they achieve them by demonstrating competence in a workplace environment.

Credit for training programmes

If you wish to arrange for recognition of your training programmes, you can still do so – but not with NVQs. A training programme can be reviewed in order to provide 'credit exemption' or 'advanced standing' (see p 148) in relation to a (non-NVQ) qualification.

This system is popular in the USA. In the UK it operates mainly in relation to degree programmes, but individual educational institutions negotiate separate arrangements with companies regarding a variety of (non-NVQ) qualifications. Should you be interested in following this further, the Council for National Academic Awards (CNAA) or your local college or polytechnic will be able to help.

One of the latest UK developments is the Investors in People Award. This links closely with NVQs. The following information section outlines the development and introduction of this award, together with its implications for employers.

✎   INFORMATION SECTION   ✎

Investors in People

The Investors in People initiative (IiP) was launched in 1990 and requires participating companies to make a 'public commitment from the top to develop all employees to achieve its business objectives'.

Delivered via Training and Enterprise Councils (TECs), the IiP initiative sets out a methodology for achieving the award which includes the establishment of a written business plan and consideration of how employees will contribute to meeting specific goals and targets. Managers and employees must regularly agree training needs and resources must be allocated.

To date, more than 400 companies have been recognised as Investors in People, while another 4000 are committed to achieving the standard.

The initiative was launched with a briefing pack, which contained three key documents. Briefing document 1 was for board members, senior managers and business development and marketing staff in Training and Enterprise Councils (Local Enterprise Councils in Scotland).

This first document provided the 'context' for the initiative, summarising the business issues which strategically drove the focus for its introduction.

The second briefing document described the framework of Investors in People and detailed the principles and action points embodied within it.

The third document was entitled 'The Proof' and provided examples of companies who were already developing their people as an investment (rather than a cost, as is traditionally the case).

The objectives of Investors in People are as follows:

To encourage companies to adopt a planned, business-led approach to investing in people, by demonstrating the business rationale for, and benefits of, this approach.

To help companies commit to investing in the people in their company, by adopting the principles and actions embodied in the national standard. Companies seeking to achieve the Investor in People status will be required to make a public commitment to this goal.

To reward companies which have met the national standard and are able to demonstrate this approach working successfully in their business. TECs and LECs are able to award a kitemark, to proclaim that a company has achieved the status of an Investor in People.

IiP briefing document 2, 1990, Employment Department

Understandably, the use of the term national standard presented some confusion when the initiative was first introduced. Most people were still getting used to 'national standards' being the basis of NVQs – and here was another 'national standard' to take on board.

Since its initial introduction, IiP has also been linked directly with NVQs and the Investors initiative is used as a means for accelerating the implementation of NVQs (and vice versa).

The initiative is based on four fundamental principles, which must be followed – it is these four principles which form the national standard for IiP:

- An Investor in People makes a public commitment from the top to develop all employees to achieve its business objectives.
- An Investor in People regularly reviews the training and development needs of all employees.
- An Investor in People takes action to train and develop individuals on recruitment and throughout their employment.
- An Investor in People evaluates the investment in training and development to assess achievement and improve future effectiveness.

Achieving the award

In order to achieve the Investors in People award, an organisation must undergo an assessment. Standards (or organisational competences) are made explicit and evidence must be provided to meet these standards. Advisers and assessors will be appointed by your local TEC/LEC.

77

Advisers and Assessors for IiP are trained (for example by Henley Management College) and must themselves achieve approved status. Once approved, IiP advisers and assessors register with a TEC/LEC and can then be allocated to companies to undertake the advisory and assessment roles.

Employers are provided with a 'diagnostic pack' and the adviser will go through the required standards and help to compile relevant evidence. An approved IiP assessor will then review this evidence. IiP Assessors are themselves judged against standards which are based on the national (NVQ) assessor standards.

An IiP assessor uses a workbook which contains all the relevant standards to be met by the organisation aiming to achieve the award. An example of the areas examined by the assessor is given below.

Investors in People – example of assessment indicator

Indicator
2.4 Responsibility for developing people is clearly identified throughout the organisation, starting at the top.

Purpose/interpretation
Establishes that responsibility is defined at all levels.

Key questions
- who is responsible for dealing with training and development matters at senior level?
- does the organisation accept the principle that managers are responsible for training and developing the staff whom they manage?
- is that responsibility clearly defined and understood?
- is it reflected in what people actually do?
- is it recognised by employees?

Investors in People, Assessor Workbook,
Employment Department, 1991

Using the above, together with notes on 'guidance' and 'typical evidence', an approved IiP assessor will review evidence presented by an organisation and record results – ultimately leading to a recommendation for the award.

Further details of the Investors in People award and how to achieve it can be obtained from your local Training and Enterprise Council, or Local Enterprise Council in Scotland. See page 214 for the address of your local TEC.

Part Two

The Practitioner's Perspective: Implementation

Part II takes you through a step-by-step approach to implementing standards and NVQs.

Step 1	Identify occupational areas	Chapter 6
Step 2	Identify standards	
Step 3	Collect information on NVQs and on available support funding	Chapter 7
Step 4	Consider implications in operational terms	
Step 5	Brief staff	Chapter 8
Step 6	Train assessors	
Step 7	Clarify certification of assessors	
Step 8	Train internal verifiers	
Step 9	Pilot first candidates/assessors	Chapter 9
Step 10	Test recording systems	
Step 11	Monitor procedures and progress	
Step 12	Plan for expansion	

—— 6 ——

Steps 1 and 2: Identification

Assuming that your company has made the decision to implement competence-based standards and NVQs, your job at the 'hands-on' end of operations now begins.

This chapter provides guidance on taking the first steps, and points you in the direction of collecting the right information, from the right people, at the right time.

So, where do you start?

Logically, if you are going to implement standards, or NVQs based on standards, you must first obtain those standards. To obtain standards, you must first decide in which occupational areas you need them. Your local Training and Enterprise Council may help with this initial research (see p 214).

STEP 1 IDENTIFYING OCCUPATIONAL AREAS

Perhaps your company has already conducted an occupational mapping exercise You may even have clear management direction about which occupations are to be used as a pilot, or as the initial implementation areas. However, let's consider implementation from the beginning and look at what needs to be done to identify these initial or pilot areas.

What is the key occupation in your organisation?

This should relate to your organisation's *key purpose* or *mission statement*.

The term 'occupation' refers to a key area of work – for example, administrative and clerical, process engineering, management, training and development: all are occupations.

It is important to recognise that occupations, as defined within the Standards Development Programme, may cross traditional boundaries of vocational training and practice. Units of competence defined for a specified occupation may be used in a number of different industries. The occupation lists included in this book are used by the Qualifications and Standards Branch at the Training, Enterprise and Education Directorate of The Employment Department (TEED) within the standards programme. The NCVQ has a slightly different listing in its database which conforms to the NCVQ framework (ie *industry-defined* standards have been constituted into units with a cross-sectoral usage).

The following list catalogues occupational areas as defined by TEED and the National Council for Vocational Qualifications. This can be used as a checklist for your organisation.

Occupational areas

Accountancy
Agriculture
Air transport
Amenity horticulture
Animal care
Architecture
Arts/performing arts
Armed forces
Baking
Banking
Basket making
Biscuit, cake, chocolate
Boat building
Blacksmiths
Books
Brushes
Building maintenance/estate
    management
Building societies
Bus and coach
Business administration
Care
Carpets

Caravanning and leisure parks
Cement
Ceramics
Chemicals
Chimney sweeps
Civil service
Clay pipes/refractories
Cleaning
Clothing
Concrete
Conservation
Construction
Cosmetics
Cotton/allied products
Crafts/enterprise
Dairy
Design
Drinks
Dry cleaners/launderers
Education
Electrical contracting
Electrical services
Electricity

Electronic office
Energy management
Engineering
Engineering construction
Engineering/profess
Envelope makers
Estate agents
Extractive industries
Fibre board/packing
Film making, TV, Video
Fire service
Flexible packaging
Floristry
Food manufacture
Footwear manufacture
Footwear repair
Forensic science
Forestry
Fresh produce
Furniture
Gamekeeping/fish husbandry
Garden/agric. machinery
Gas
Glass
Guidance/counselling
Hairdressing
Hand/machine knitting
Health and beauty
Health and safety
Horses
Hotel and catering
Housing
Information technology
IT – constructive users
IT – practitioners
Inland waterways
Insurance
International trade
Jewellery

Knitting and lace
Languages
Law
Leather processing
Light leathergoods
Leather – saddle/bridle
Local government
Locksmiths
Management/supervisory
Man-made fibres
Merchant navy
Meat
Millers
Mining (including coke)
Museums, galleries/heritage
Narrow fabrics
Newspapers
Nuclear
Office skills
Offshore oil
Packaging
Paint
Paper and board
Pensions management
Periodicals
Personnel management
Petrol refining
Pharmaceuticals
Photography
Plastics
Police
Ports and harbours
Post Office
Printing
Printing ink
Prisons
Purchasing and supply
Railways
Retail

Retail travel	Sugar
Road transport	Telecommunications
Rubber	Textile manufacture
Sales	Thatching
Screen printers	Theatre technicians
Sea fishing	Timber
Security	Tobacco
Shipbuilding	Tourism and leisure
Signmaking	Training and development
Soap and detergent	Wall covering
Small businesses	Wastes management
Small tool/plant hire	Water
Sound	Wholesale
Sport and recreation	Wire and wire rope
Steel	Wool

The above list includes occupational areas where Industry Lead Bodies (see Chapter 1) have been established. If you are unsure of a direct connection with any of the above, refer to the Lead Body section in Part III.

What are the key occupational roles within your organisation?

This question may present a little more difficulty, as it requires a shift of thinking. The traditional way of thinking about standards is to relate them to *jobs* – but the same job can have many different titles. In addition, there are many jobs within an *occupation*.

The usual source of information regarding work roles within an organisation is the personnel department. You will need to review the information available – but be careful about using job descriptions or job specifications since these outline individual job titles, not occupational roles.

Examples of occupational roles may include supervisor, technician, operative or trainer.

Remember, when considering key occupational roles, to think in broader terms than the key occupation of your organisation. The key occupation may be manufacturing, or processing, or one of the service industries, but key occupational roles will include the *range* and levels of activity undertaken within the organisation.

What supporting occupations occur within your organisation?

To make sure that you include all organisational activities, don't forget to list the managerial, administrative or unskilled roles that support your organisation's main function. If you work in a very large company, many different roles contribute to effective operations.

Are you introducing standards across the board or in key occupations only?

Having established a clear 'occupational map', you now need to be clear about which occupational areas to address first. In general, organisations tend to introduce competence-based standards and NVQs in the key occupational areas (and key occupational roles) for the initial, pilot phase. In this way, the contribution to improved performance can be judged directly in relation to key areas of performance. However, supporting occupations can also play a key part in successful performance, and your company's decision will be based on consideration of implications and benefits in relation to operational objectives.

STEP 2 IDENTIFYING STANDARDS

Once you know the occupational areas in which you will be introducing standards and NVQs, the next problem is *finding* the standards.

Current work on development of national standards is gradually ensuring that these will be available in all occupational areas, but some sectors are way ahead of others. You need to find the answers to two key questions: Are national standards available for the identified key occupational areas? And how do these national standards relate to our needs?

Should the answer to the first of these be no, you then have to consider the following options: Do we wait until relevant national standards become available? Do we start work on our own competence-based standards? Are there draft national standards available which we can use as a foundation for our own developments? If we develop our own standards, how can we ensure that we can still link in with new NVQs when they become available?

Taking each of these questions in turn we'll consider

- how to get information
- what to do with the information when you have it
- implications of action.

Are national standards available for the identified key occupational areas?

In order to answer this question, you need to check with the providers of national standards – the Industry Lead Body or with the providers of qualifications which incorporate these standards – the awarding bodies. This can be done in one of three ways:

- contact the Industry Lead Body direct
- access the NCVQ database
- contact the awarding body.

You should not contact the NCVQ direct for information on standards.

A full list of current Industry Lead Bodies is provided in Part III, together with addresses, contact names and telephone numbers.

The NCVQ database is available on disc for access through a desk-top computer. It contains detailed information on all NVQs including the component units, elements and performance criteria and range statements (see Chapter 3 for explanations of these terms). The contact for obtaining the database is given in Part III.

If standards are still under development, the awarding bodies will be involved in this work. In England and Wales the major awarding bodies are City and Guilds (C&G), the Business and Technology Education Council (BTEC), the Royal Society of Arts (RSA) and a wide range of professional bodies. In Scotland, the sole awarding body is the Scottish Vocational Education Council (Scotvec). Each has a publicity/information section and a catalogue of its qualifications. First identify the relevant awarding body from their catalogue of occupational qualifications and then contact their information office for details. Addresses are given in Part III.

Your choice of approach will depend upon whether your company is planning to introduce NVQs as its key objective, or if your key interest is in *standards*. The NCVQ database lists only those NVQs which have been officially accredited (ie after a contract between the relevant parties and the NCVQ has been signed). If you want to know the current state of play regarding development of standards (which will form the basis of new NVQs), then your best contact would be the Industry Lead Body. TEED also publishes *The Standards Digest* (see Part III for details). This lists current developments in standards and NVQs by occupations and is available to those people involved in the development of standards.

Let's assume that you have identified national standards (and NVQs) through the NCVQ database and/or through the Industry Lead Body. As all national standards are published by Lead Bodies, you can obtain a hard copy of the relevant standards and assessment guidance and check their applicability within your own organisation. This brings us to the next question.

How do these national standards relate to our needs?

National standards of occupational competence are developed to provide a benchmark of competent performance within a specified sector. Some developments, such as management competences or those for the training and development fields, are more 'generic' in nature; that is, they are used within a wide range of industry and commercial sectors. However, they will have been developed and tested through consultation with key role holders within defined areas of competence.

A key point about this sector-specific development relates both to mobility and exchangeability of the workforce. By introducing a common standard across each sector (and ensuring that the quality of assessment to those standards is maintained), it should be possible to create an employment environment in which recruitment, selection, manpower planning etc can be conducted on a common basis. Instead of having different standards between regions, or between companies, employers will be able to use the new certification (qualification) scheme as a hallmark of individuals' achievements.

Some companies have found, however, that the benchmark of competence, while serving the 'exchangeability' function quite adequately, is not sufficient for their own corporate purposes. Reasons for this perceived inadequacy include:

- the desire to incorporate the company's mission statement and objectives into operational standards
- the organisation's specific culture
- the organisation's commitment to excellence
- previously specified company standards.

87

This is not to say that new competence-based standards are not applicable – simply that they may need 'enhancing' or 'contextualising' in order to meet the organisational requirements.

There is no reason why this cannot be done, as long as the enhanced standards use the national standards as a core and retain the same format. Similarly, the associated assessment system must retain its quality and meet national criteria – as well as your company's operational needs. It is quite likely, therefore, that you will need help in achieving this contextualisation. This is a cost implication that must be considered.

You may, of course, decide that the published national standards completely meet your needs, and that you can introduce the units of competence (see Chapter 3) as they stand. If this is the case, you are in the lucky position of being able to move forward to the next chapter!

It is probably fair to say, however, that having identified the published standards for relevant occupational areas and roles, some difficulties will be encountered. Some units may be completely relevant while others are not.

There is no reason why you should introduce *all* the units from a defined NVQ. There is no point in trying to assess people in areas of work for which they have no responsibility, interest or even skill. The point of a credit-accumulation system is that units of competence are accessible individually. The NVQ framework will combine a number of units into a qualification. Your company may wish to introduce a mixture of units from a range of occupational roles – and even to negotiate with an awarding body to establish a new NVQ in a specialised area.

Perhaps the best way to illustrate this point is with an example. The feature from London Fire Brigade (p 90) shows shows how a large organisation with specialised needs is making use of existing published standards and meeting its own particular operational requirements.

What if national standards and/or NVQs are not yet available? Do we wait until relevant national standards become available?

The latter question can only be answered in relation to your company's reasons for introducing competence-based standards. What is the senior management directive on this issue? How urgent is the introduction of standards? For what reasons?

Much will depend on the current state of play in standards development. You can contact the Industry Lead Body for an up-to-date picture and proposed timescales for production of national standards. This will at least provide you with the basis on which to make an informed decision.

If an Industry Lead Body has not yet been established (this will be mainly in small or very specialised sectors), you can contact the Training, Enterprise and Education Directorate Qualifications and Standards Branch at Moorfoot in Sheffield for information. The TEED has its own database for progress on standards development. The Qualifications and Standards Branch has personnel assigned to each sector of industry and commerce.

Do we start work on our own competence-based standards?

You can do so, if the company is willing to invest time and money. You may already have company standards which you feel are competence-based. However, you should make sure you are familiar with the basic concepts and methodology involved in developing national competence-based standards (see Part I), before you make assumptions that your standards are in line with current developments.

The costs of development need careful consideration. Chapter 5 illustrated some of the cost headings involved in the development of national standards.

Are there draft national standards available which we can use as a foundation for our own developments?

This is quite likely to be the case. The Industry Lead Body (or TEED as above) will be able to provide you with information. You should note, however, that most Lead Bodies are reluctant to release draft versions of standards. This is because of the obvious assumption that providers and employers would use them for development of assessment and training programmes, only to find that the final, published version is drastically different!

You should therefore ensure that any draft material you intend to use has been field tested on at least one occasion.

Should you decide to take the route of developing your own company standards, it is likely that you will need consultancy support. Make sure you use a consultant who is fully *au fait* with national developments, including the technicalities of methodology. Taking a diverse (if cheaper) route can be less cost-effective in the long run.

If we develop our own standards, how can we ensure that we can still link in with new NVQs when they become available?

There is no reason why in-company standards (and assessment systems) should not meet national criteria, provided that careful liaison with national developments is maintained during the development process.

Awarding bodies need to be involved in the development stage; most will work with companies to establish a tailor-made qualification (this is essential in highly specialised areas anyway). For an example of this type of work, take a look at the London Fire Brigade case study at the end of Chapter 6.

As you may have gathered by now, identifying occupational areas and standards is a key activity in the introduction of competence-based systems for measuring, monitoring and rewarding performance in the workplace. If standards are the foundation for improvement of performance then the foundation must be solid before any further action can be taken.

Chapter 7 looks at preparing the organisation. This can only be done when you are clear about the nature of the standards which you intend to introduce.

Get the standards right before taking any further action!

■ CASE STUDY ■

London Fire Brigade

London Fire Brigade employs over 4,000 firefighters at recruit, probationer and firefighter levels. Operating over five areas with an HQ in South London, the Brigade, with a total of nearly 8,000 uniformed and non-uniformed staff, provides an operational and fire safety service to the London private and business population.

In line with developments in most public sector organisations, the Brigade is undergoing radical management changes. These include preparing for competitive tendering and monitoring and assessing the performance of firefighters. It is proposed that the traditional hierarchical structure is *flattened* to provide a more efficient and effective work-force.

However, these changes, whilst akin to those undertaken in many major organisations during the 1990s, pose a dilemma for management. The hierarchical command structure of a uniformed service is critical if it is to work in the life-threatening environment of the firefighter. On the other hand, in operational support, management and fire safety, such a multi-layered structure can be a disadvantage – it can discourage individual responsibility and initiative.

The Brigade is constantly reviewing its performance, not simply in terms of response times, which are governed by Home Office guidelines, but also in terms of the competent performance of its workforce. Recent developments have focused on further improvement in levels of competence, combined with structural changes to encourage and develop empowerment of employees.

A review of training undertaken by the Brigade has been underway for some time. The objectives (are):

- to ensure that all personnel are properly trained in operational techniques and procedures
- to create a culture within the authority where quality of service is the priority and where the performance and contributions of groups and individuals can be identified, measured and rewarded
- to develop the authority as an organisation where staff are given the opportunity to learn and develop in a supportive organisational environment where initiative is encouraged
- to develop and maintain a structured programme to ensure that sufficient staff are available with the skills, knowledge and experience necessary to meet the authority's current and future needs.
- to develop and implement a programme to identify staff with managerial potential and to develop and train those staff in order to meet the authority's identified needs.

In developing all proposals for training activities a functional approach was taken. By determining the expectations of its staff at work, the training that would be needed to support that performance became much clearer.

The Brigade recognised that, in order to design competence-based training it must first clearly state exactly **what** it wanted its workforce to do and **how well** it wanted them to do it. With this in mind, a consultancy project, called the Operational Competences Project, was commissioned.

This project provided a team of 15 officers with training and a methodology to develop competence-based standards of performance for all areas of the firefighting and rescue service, including the supporting management and administration functions. Competences for all staff were developed through wide consultation and validation across all of the relevant areas of the Brigade.

These developments were closely linked to those at national level – where occupational standards were also under development. Whilst the Brigade was keen to ensure a match with these national developments, the main priority of the Operational Competences Project was to meet the specific needs of London Fire Brigade, in a time frame which did not fit with the national development schedule.

In addition the competences, once developed, were structured into units and this unit structure used for 'mapping' the future role of the Brigade. Thus the unit structure provided a flexible basis on which to establish and review the expectations of new roles and the progression routes between them.

Close liaison with the training and development function is enabling the operational competences to be used as the basis for training design. Further developments will include the design and implementation of an assessment system, using the competences as a foundation for all forms of assessing competent performance.

Thus the Brigade is using a competence framework as a tool for change. Working groups are examining the key roles in the Brigade; the competences are defining exactly what each role and function is in terms of what the Brigade expects from each individual and the performance measures to be used for assessment. Should restructuring of roles be necessary in the future – in order to meet operational demands – the Brigade now has a flexible tool to achieve this, by reorganising functional 'units' into a new combination.

This links directly to a qualitative performance scheme introduced through an Operations and Training Performance Inspectorate. Ultimately, performance will be split into a number of levels to include:

- The performance of staff assessed in training, on exercises and at incidents.
- Brigade management, responsible, for example, for assessing how well a new policy on new equipment has been introduced.

Mr Brian Robinson, Chief Fire Officer, is leading these changes and believes these will ensure that London Fire Brigade is ready to meet the challenges of the future. 'Performance management is not about blame, it is about support to people in the organisation by ensuring that our training and development mechanisms are validated and targeted to the places that matter'.

Steps 3 and 4: Preparing the Organisation or Department

STEP 3 COLLECTING INFORMATION ON NVQS

Once you have established the nature of the competence-based standards you are going to introduce, you are ready to consider the implications of their introduction.

If you are also introducing NVQs (with national standards as their base) you will be ready to collect information on these qualifications from the awarding bodies, which may include the relevant Industry Lead Body itself (see Chapter 1).

Each NVQ will have specific requirements attached relating to the assessment process. For example, some NVQs have a requirement for workplace assessors to be 'registered' or licensed. Some may supply documentation for recording assessment as part of the initial registration fee. Check on the costs of such materials.

You may be introducing a full NVQ (ie all units of a specified qualification) or units of more than one full NVQ, but all NVQs will include arrangements for quality control – referred to as 'verification' or 'moderation'. An *internal* verifier is a designated person within the company who monitors the work of in-company assessors (often supervisors or first-line managers). An *external* verifier is an awarding body representative who will visit a sample of companies on a regular basis to ensure that standards are being maintained and that the assessment system is operating as it should. (See section on The Common Accord p 171).

The costs of verification are often built in to the NVQ operational system. They may be included in an initial registration fee, or in annual operating costs. You should ask for clarification of all costs involved.

'Certification' refers to the award of certificates to successful candidates. This usually involves a separate fee and can be charged on a unit certificate basis (usually around £6 per unit), or on a full NVQ basis (usually between £35–£125 per certificate). You should clarify whether fees include issue of an NVQ certificate. Awarding bodies have their own system of charging for their own certificates, and the NCVQ also have a certification charge.

What to ask about NVQs

- What are the requirements for assessment of units?
- Are there specific requirements for
  - training of assessors
  - registration of assessors?
  - costs?
- Is there an initial registration fee?
- If so, what does this registration fee cover?
- Is the registration fee payable annually?
- Is there an 'assessment centre approval process' attached to registration? Does this meet the requirements of the Common Accord?
- What are verification and moderation arrangements?
- Are there any hidden costs involved?
- What are the arrangements for certification of successful candidates?
- What are the certification fees?
- Is there any separate arrangement for assessment of knowledge and understanding?
- Is there a procedure for accreditation of prior learning?

STEP 4 CONSIDER THE IMPLICATIONS IN OPERATIONAL TERMS

Introducing competence-based standards and NVQs will have a direct impact on the training culture within your organisation.

Systems of workplace assessment require commitment and involvement. Learning programmes will need to be revised or developed to contribute towards achievement of required standards. Staff will take on new roles and responsibilities – a point to note when discussing changes with trades unions.

You might think of the introduction of competence-based standards and NVQs as a programme for change. Like all change programmes, it will require careful planning to ensure that the staff resources and expertise are available, and that the new actions for change will influence company operations only in a positive sense.

You will need to establish an in-company assessment model. This means considering who will be designated assessors and how they will assess. Who will train assessors and how will they be trained? What costs are involved in this activity? Does the awarding body or Industry Lead Body specify a training programme or can you develop one of your own? Will your assessors gain qualifications in assessment? Is this a requirement?

You must also consider *quality control*. Who will be designated as internal verifier? Who will be the key contact for introducing standards and NVQs? Who will liaise with awarding bodies regarding external verification and certification?

You will also need to consider training implications. Who will be responsible for ensuring training contributes to achievement of standards? When will training programmes be developed? How will training delivery be affected?

If this sounds like a great deal of work – it is! Any programme for change requires considerable effort and it is essential that all roles and responsibilities are clarified before implementation begins.

The checklists below will help you with some of the key questions you need to consider at this vital planning stage.

Introducing standards and NVQs – initial checklist

Does your organisation have

- a clear training policy?
- a clear training strategy?
- a plan for implementing standards and NVQs?
- a senior staff member designated with responsibility for implementation?
- job descriptions which outline training responsibilities?
- a staff appraisal system?

- a system for forecasting staffing needs?
- an agreed culture?
- existing company qualifications?
- existing reward/incentive schemes?
- existing arrangements with awarding bodies/educational institutions for award of qualifications?
- existing continuous assessment schemes?
- company-defined learning/training programmes?
- company-defined standards?
- selection/recruitment policies linked to job descriptions?

All or any of the above activities can influence, or be influenced by, the introduction of competence-based standards and NVQs. In order to understand the implications and benefits of each activity, you must have a clear understanding of the concepts and principles of these new developments, and of the specific operational requirements of the NVQs you intend to introduce.

If you decide you need help to plan the introduction of standards and NVQs, Industry Lead Bodies and awarding bodies can provide guidance. Consultancy help is also available, but make sure you check that your chosen source of help is fully cognisant of developments and is able to consider the application of these developments within your specific company context.

Introducing standards and NVQs – staff role checklist

Management responsibility
Who is responsible for

- implementing standards/NVQs at
  - organisational level?
  - departmental level?
- liaison with awarding bodies?
- monitoring effectiveness of new systems?
- arranging development of competence-based training programmes?

Operational responsibility
Who is responsible for

- initial assessment procedures (including assessment of prior learning)?

- assessing candidates' performance at work and recording assessment?
- monitoring (verifying) assessors' work including counter-signing assessments?
- identifying training needs?
- preparing training plans?

Trades unions

A brief note regarding discussions with trades unions is essential. By now, you are probably fully aware that the introduction of competence-based standards and NVQs can have far-reaching implications and benefits for your organisation.

Not least of these is the potential perceived change in staff roles and responsibilities. For those companies who have introduced total quality management, or BS5750, or some form of total quality system, the idea of line management's greater involvement in the development and assessment of staff will not come as any great shock. In fact, competence-based standards should serve to make explicit what supervisors and line managers are doing on a daily basis anyway – continuously assessing the performance of staff for whom they have direct responsibility.

However, the introduction of assessment recording systems, on an individual basis, is likely to be met by a wide range of reactions that you must be prepared to deal with. No doubt trades unions will want to question the changes in roles and responsibilities – the introduction of NVQs, with external recognition for work performance, is a form of reward or incentive system.

Some of the issues which may arise will relate to existing incentive schemes (or previous ones). Others may relate to the fact that assessors are being given responsibility for 'signing off competence'. This latter issue may be particularly problematic in sectors where health and safety is a key issue. For example, what happens if a line manager/supervisor 'signs off' an employee as competent in installing a delicate or potentially dangerous piece of equipment and something goes wrong with that equipment?

This will be a valid and pertinent point to be addressed in many industries, as will issues pertaining to incentive and reward. But there is no universal guidance on these matters. Careful planning through consideration of all the issues outlined in this and the previous chapter will help you prepare for such discussions.

Accreditation of prior learning

This integral part of competence-based assessment is covered in more detail in Chapter 11, but needs mention here in relation to forward planning.

The accreditation of prior learning (APL) permits the award of credit towards a qualification on the basis of evidence drawn from an individual's past achievements. For companies, this means that you can use the APL assessment process to take a skills audit of your staff and provide them with credit towards an NVQ as recognition of their current level of competence.

An additional benefit for you is that, having completed this assessment, training needs will have been clearly identified, on both individual and group bases, and future training can be targeted to those areas where it is really needed. This will obviously save time and provide a more cost-effective training solution as well as providing motivation for staff to be both assessed and trained.

The major awarding bodies have developed and agreed policies for the operation of APL in connection with a wide range of qualifications. However, procedures for operating the APL process within all occupational areas have not yet been finalised. You will therefore need to check that procedures are in place within the relevant occupational areas.

The costs involved will include a fee for verification (paid to the awarding body) and training of assessors. Given the overall benefits of operating APL as an initial assessment process, this is a cost-effective means of introducing NVQs.

The responsibility for collecting evidence of competence (to match the specified standards) rests with individual candidates. You may need to allow time for your staff to do this.

Further information on APL is included in Chapter 11; copies of awarding bodies' guidance and policy is available on request from their central offices.

Once again, should you need help to introduce APL, check that your source of help is fully cognisant with the concepts, principles and operational requirements involved. The following information section provides advice on one possible support initiative – see also the section on TECs (p 112).

❧ INFORMATION SECTION ❧

Skill Choice

The Skill Choice initiative, which was announced in the White Paper, *People, Jobs and Opportunities*, in February 1992, is a significant element of the Training, Enterprise and Education Directorate's Individual Commitment Strategy which seeks to persuade individuals that training pays and to take responsibility for their own career development. The initiative aims to:

- develop effective and comprehensive information, assessment and guidance services for people who are primarily in work;
- put individual people in the driving seat by offering them credits which they can use to buy the guidance and assessment services of their choice.

TECs/LECs are involved, with the intention that 250,000 people will benefit over two years 1993/94 and 1994/95. The Government has stated that if assessment and guidance credits are successful and cost-effective, it intends to make them available across the country.

Each TEC/LEC involved is required to secure the development of a network of local assessment and guidance services – this builds on previous initiatives such as Gateway and Access to Assessment. The initiative then offers a significant contribution towards the cost and assessment and guidance from a range of providers accredited by the TEC/LEC.

The Skill Choice initiative was introduced in April 1993.

How can it help you?

The Skill Choice initiative offers funding towards guidance, assessment and accreditation for individuals aiming to achieve NVQs. Employers can access this funding for their employees.

Employers are required to submit a proposal to their local TEC illustrating the number of people involved, the relevant NVQs, how action and assessment planning will be undertaken and the number of NVQs (or units towards them) that will be achieved within a given timescale.

Once funding support is approved, the employer must submit (monthly) details of action/assessment plans agreed and accreditations achieved. A percentage of funding is then provided per individual.

Each participating TEC (15 in England in 1993) and LEC (4 in Scotland in 1993) has to reach its target figure for action plans, assessment plans and accreditations, so working with employers is advantageous to TECs and LECs and large numbers go through.

TECs can also provide help with identification of approved providers who can assist with planning and implementation. These developments can also be linked to other TEC supported initiatives such as Investors in People (see page 76) and Business Change, Gateway, or Business Development schemes.

Contact your local TEC for more information. A full list of TECs with addresses and telephone numbers is included in pages 214-226.

——8——

Steps 5 to 8: Staff Briefing and Development

STEP 5 STAFF BRIEFING

Once you have a plan for the introduction of competence-based standards and NVQs, you need to consider how to communicate those plans to everyone involved.

Much will depend upon your implementation plan, but it is usually a good idea to consider an organisational briefing which outlines the reasons behind the decision to introduce new developments, together with the benefits to both the organisation and the individual.

You might consider using an existing staff newsletter, or networking structures to cascade information. Alternatively, a special staff briefing might be arranged. Whatever your choice, consider the following points for inclusion in a major briefing exercise:

- reasons why standards and NVQs are being introduced
- explanation of what standards and NVQs are
- description of areas they are being introduced in
- details of the order they are being introduced – and why
- how the company will benefit from the introduction
- how individuals will benefit from the introduction
- trade union support
- what the introduction means in terms of staff roles and responsibilities
- when the first implementation will start
- how it will be monitored
- procedures for people to communicate ideas and feed-back

■ request for applications for first candidates (if you are conducting a pilot scheme first).

Staff development

Companies have been quick to realise the potential flexibility that competence-based standards offer to the training function. With explicit and measurable standards of expected performance which can be made available to everyone who uses them, the design and delivery of training becomes less hit and miss and more directly targeted to individual and group and company needs.

However, as companies begin to introduce new competence-based standards and NVQs, they are also beginning to realise the importance of staff development, particularly for assessors.

Most of us have a particular perception of assessment. The traditional view was outlined in Part I. If you are unclear about the principles and concepts of competence-based assessment, and how they differ from the more traditional approach, you should read through Chapter 4 before continuing with this section.

NVQ assessment model

All NVQS operate within a defined assessment model (see Figure 8.1). Assessment is determined by the elements of competence, range statements and performance criteria which form the standards of competence. Assessment itself is a process of obtaining evidence and making judgements about that evidence.

The key form of assessment within NVQs is therefore observation of performance. However, this is not always possible, particularly in the case of various contingencies or health-and-safety-hazardous environments.

Assessors operating within competence-based systems must therefore be fully aware of various methods of assessment and their use within the workplace if they are to assess the full specified range of activities. (Further detailed discussion of competence-based assessment will be found in Chapter 11.)

STEP 6 ASSESSOR TRAINING

One particular danger of introducing competence-based standards and NVQs is the tendency to assume that people already know about

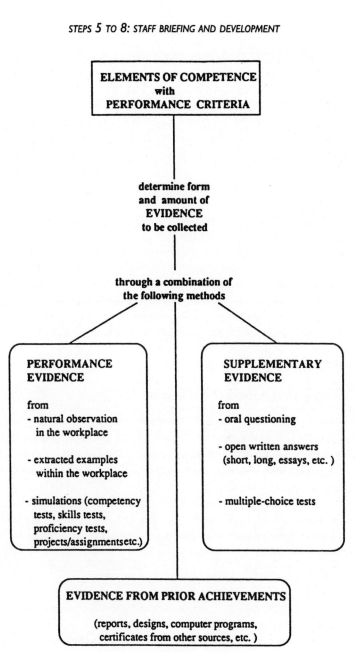

Figure 8.1 The NVQ assessment model

assessment. After all, isn't competence-based assessment only making explicit what supervisors and line managers do anyway?

This is true, although perhaps it would be more accurate to say that competence-based assessment makes explicit what supervisors and line managers *should* be doing anyway! How consistent is continuous assessment in your organisation? How good are your line managers at recognising and reporting training needs, or completing annual appraisals?

While we may all have a good idea of what assessment is, when it comes to actually doing it we find that our ideas are not the same as those held by the people we have to assess, or by our colleagues who have to conduct a similar assessment.

The point of introducing competence-based systems is to gain *consistency*. Consistent maintenance of standards, both in performance and assessment, can contribute to development of performance. It is important to recognise, therefore, that *training of workplace assessors* is vital to the successful implementation and operation of competence-based systems. Quality assurance requirements now include a demand that assessors and verifiers achieve national accreditation – see p 173 for details.

Training programmes for assessors

Workplace assessors need to be competent in their assessment role. You may find that the awarding bodies for the NVQs which you plan to introduce offer assessor-training programmes. The benefits of these are that they are usually sector-specific and deal with issues arising from the particular NVQ.

However, with a focus on quality of assessors, you should check that the assessor training will meet your operational requirements and national criteria for approval when accredited and that it includes the following:

- basic concepts of competence-based assessment
- issues of evidence of competence
- assessor skills, including use of various methods of assessment
- maintaining quality of assessment
- procedures and processes for assessment of performance and for assessment of knowledge and understanding (these are sometimes separate, eg financial services sector)
- procedures for accreditation of prior learning, including issues of

evidence from past achievements
- verification/moderation procedures
- recording procedures and documentation
- certification procedures
- appeals procedures

You may find that the content or the duration of assessor training courses on offer do not meet your operational needs. You may choose to develop and deliver your own in-company programme, or to use external consultants to do this for you. Various open learning packages are also available. Once again, the issue of making sure that your selected consultant is *au fait* with developments and key concepts is a paramount issue.

STEP 7 CERTIFICATION FOR ASSESSORS

Awarding bodies have overall responsibility for assessment in connection with NVQs because they award the final certificates. You may therefore find requirements for 'registration' of assessors. There will also be a requirement for assessors to achieve a recognised qualification. You can arrange this through liaison with an awarding body (or your external consultant could take care of this for you). This will, of course, involve your in-company assessors undergoing assessment. (The terminology gets confusing – who assesses assessors?!)

This need not be complicated. All your in-company assessors will be monitored by an internal and an external verifier (see p 55 for explanations of these terms). Assessors will therefore be demonstrating competence in their assessment role on an ongoing basis – in the same way as the people they are assessing are demonstrating competence in their work roles. Assistance with funding for this development is available from Training and Enterprise Councils (TECs) (see p 112).

STEP 8 INTERNAL VERIFIER TRAINING

Internal verifiers are in-company staff responsible for monitoring assessment. They may also have a role as 'countersigning officers' – responsible for signing the assessment documentation to support the decision of the first-line assessor. Verifiers will need to understand the basic concepts, principles and procedures of competence-based assessment in the same depth as first-line assessors. They will also need to be clear about the verifier's role and liaison with awarding bodies. (See p 247 for TEC financial assistance.)

Accreditation of prior learning (APL)

Once again, a separate note on this issue, although it is an integral part of competence-based assessment.

If you are planning to introduce APL, you will have included training in this form of assessment in your initial assessor training package. It is essential to the credibility of the assessment system that assessors are aware of issues relating to evidence from past achievements and can provide quality guidance to candidates. (A brief discussion of these issues is provided in Chapter 11.)

A question of choice

When introducing competence-based standards and NVQs, your company can choose whether to use nationally agreed standards of competence as they stand, or to enhance or 'contextualise' them to meet organisational demands. Similarly, you can choose to make use of the assessor training packages available to you or to develop your own. These decisions must be based on a review of the specific NVQs you plan to introduce.

—9—

Steps 9 to 12: Starting, Maintaining and Expanding the system

STEP 9 PILOT FIRST CANDIDATES AND ASSESSORS

When your initial training programmes are complete, you are ready to start your first assessments. Remember, these are not traditional assessment procedures of a one-off nature, your in-company assessment scheme will operate on a continuous day-by-day basis.

Briefing the candidates

All candidates for assessment should be fully briefed about the assessment system. They should have easy access to the standards at all times – and to their assessor.

The designated assessor (usually a line manager), who may be responsible for several candidates (usually his own staff), should meet with the candidate and ensure that a clear *assessment plan is agreed.*

Assessment plans

The purpose of an assessment plan is to set parameters for both candidate and assessor. Both need to be clear on *what* is being assessed and *how* it is being assessed.

As competence-based assessment focuses on evidence of performance, assessor and candidate can decide what forms of evidence are most likely to be created in the normal work pattern of the candidate.

The assessor and candidate will need to agree which *units of competence* the candidate will be aiming to achieve. They can also agree a timescale for assessment. Figure 9.1 illustrates a typical process for agreeing an assessment plan. Such a plan will be a requirement if you are seeking funding from TECs to assist with your implementation.

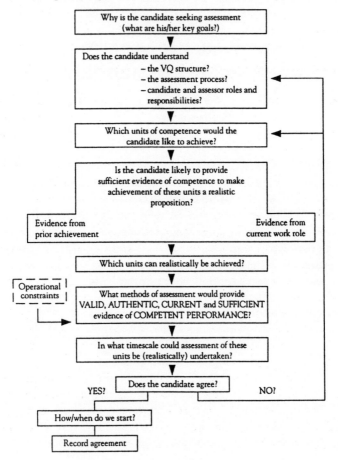

Figure 9.1 A typical assessment plan process

Assessor support

Assessors will need support, not only to help them in the role, but also to ensure that standards are maintained. A networking system, allowing assessors to meet on a regular basis, would enable a forum for exchange of ideas and mutual support to be established.

Regular meetings with internal verifiers and external verifiers should also be encouraged. These arrangements will obviously need to fit in with operational requirements, but the importance of assessor support to general maintenance of a quality assessment system should not be underestimated.

STEP 10 OPERATE RECORDING SYSTEMS

You may find that the NVQs you are implementing are supported by documentation for recording assessment. If so, the initial introduction to the NVQ, both in briefing and training stages, should outline the use of this documentation.

In general, there is no reason why you cannot operate your own recording system, particularly if you find that the one offered by the awarding body(ies) does not meet your day-to-day operational needs. However, you should ensure that any recording system includes clear guidance for assessors (as a general reference point) and also allows sufficient space for recording of evidence presented, and signatures of assessor, verifier and candidate.

Documentation relating to assessment must be kept up to date and available for verifiers to review. Assessment documentation and evidence collected can be used for final assessment, particularly where evidence from past achievement is included. Any collection of evidence by a single candidate can be compiled into a 'portfolio' which serves as an assessment document in itself.

The assessor is responsible for recording the results of assessment. Records should be maintained legibly and accurately and be accessible to candidate, assessor, assessor-colleagues and verifiers. However, confidentiality between candidate and those staff with legitimate access to records must be maintained.

STEP 11 MONITOR PROCEDURES AND PROGRESS

The internal and external verifiers will be responsible for monitoring of the assessors and the assessment system. However, maintenance of standards is a key issue for your company – consistency of performance through the introduction of standards is one of the key reasons for introducing competence-based standards.

You may wish to introduce your own monitoring system, perhaps using the external verifier as a source of information, as he/she will have a general overview of the progress of a number of candidates and a number of assessors.

Specific questions you may consider include:

- How is the assessor/candidate ratio working out?
- Are assessors able to cope with the number of candidates?
- Are assessors/candidates having any difficulties with
  - types of evidence required?
  - organisation of workload to produce range of evidence required?
  - coping with assessment documentation?

In addition to monitoring the actual assessment system, you will also want to consider measures of effectiveness as the first part of your evaluation of the new system's contribution to improved performance.

The measures you may choose to use in this respect will be similar to those used to evaluate the effectiveness of training:

- increased productivity
- lower absenteeism
- lower level of complaints
- decreased reject rate.

It is probably a good idea to begin compiling your overall evaluation plan at this stage. By using initial information on progress you will begin to formulate a clear idea of the most appropriate measures to apply.

STEP 12 PLAN FOR EXPANSION

When your pilot programme is running smoothly, you will need to consider plans for expansion. The following questions might be considered:

- How many more candidates for assessment do we have in this occupational area?
- Do we have adequate numbers of assessors?
- How can we phase training of assessors and introduction of assessment across all staff in this occupational area?

- What will be the next occupational area in which we will introduce NVQs?
- Are there any differences between operational requirements for NVQ in the second occupational area?
- What difficulties have arisen in this first area that we can also foresee in the next?
- What solutions have we tried/have worked/can we forecast for new areas?

Importance of maintaining standards

As we have already noted on several occasions in these last few chapters, perhaps the biggest benefit for companies introducing competence-based standards and assessment is the potential for *consistency* of performance.

Achieving consistency requires commitment – commitment to effective training and to quality control. All of this requires time and effort on the part of everyone involved.

Most companies have found that the early stages of introduction throw up a range of difficulties, mainly because people are attempting to adjust not only to a new way of working but also to a new way of *thinking*.

Focusing on performance, and on the *outcomes of performance*, requires a shift in thinking. Using new forms of assessment, developing new skills, and taking responsibility for new forms of record keeping all involve a 'learning curve'. Results will not be immediate and no doubt there will be complaints of 'time wasting record keeping' and 'irrelevance' during the first few months.

Getting help

The following information section provides an outline of the operation of Training and Enterprise Councils (TECs) – one source of help for introducing and/or expanding NVQ operation in your company.

❧ INFORMATION SECTION ☙

What are TECs and why do they exist?

It was a White Paper, 'Employment for the 1990s' (*HMSO, 1988*) which proposed the establishment of Training and Enterprise Councils (TECs) in England and Wales and Local Enterprise Councils (LECs) in Scotland. The timescale for this new development was made clear: 'The Government expect that a national network of TECs will evolve gradually over a period of three to four years'. The philosophy behind this proposal was that:

> each community must shape a clear vision stretching beyond exist-ing programmes, organisation and methods of delivery. It must place education, training and enterprise in the broader context of economic and industrial development.

The establishment of TECs and LECs was based on five major princi-ples of reform:

- A locally based system.
- An employer-led partnership.
- A focused approach.
- An accent on performance.
- An enterprise organisation.
  (Employment Department, 1990)

It was envisaged that the first prospective TECs would enter their development phases in July 1989 and a transition to full TEC opera-tion would occur in April 1990, with up to 60 TECs operational or ready to become operational by July 1990. A full list of TECs and their operational dates are included in the Appendix.

The funding provided for TEC expenditure on the development phase was initially limited to £11 million. The overall management, control and direction of work associated with TECs rested with the Director General of the Training Agency, who was supported by a formal Project Board. Action Managers were appointed with respon-sibility for co-ordinating, monitoring and reporting on each block of work involved in the TEC Project. Issue Managers were also appointed and were responsible for delivery of particular products or outputs. Project Management Guidelines were issued and the Project Management Unit managed progress reports. TECs are independent companies, each having a contract with the Secretary of State for Employment. They are normally limited by guarantee and run by a Board of Directors. (The original requirement, as stated in the prospectus (*Employment Department, 1993*), was that two-thirds of its board would be private sector employers at Chief Executive or Managing Director level, the rest being drawn from leaders of education, economic development, trade unions, voluntary organisations and the public sector). The key focus was that they should be run by business leaders and aim to provide the country with the skilled and enterprising workforce needed for sustained growth and prosperity. By the end of 1992 (last available figures) it was estimated that 1085 businesses and community leaders were involved with TECs in England.

The TEC Project, led by the Training Agency, aimed to co-ordinate the planning, management and delivery of TEC implementation. The scope of the Project included all efforts associated with establishing:

- a full network of operational TECs in England and Wales with appropriate support arrangements
- a platform for the growth of TEC responsibilities towards a role for TECs at the heart of local economic development.

The Training Agency established a Project Management Unit to take forward this planning and implementation. The TECs were set Strategic Priorities (which have not changed). Since these were set, quantitative measures have been clarified in terms of the National Education and Training Targets.

TEC/LEC STRATEGIC PRIORITIES

- Encourage effective employer investment in skills, and stimulate employers to meet the lifetime learning targets.
- Help young people achieve their full potential, and raise attainment in line with the foundation learning targets.
- Stimulate individuals to take responsibility for their own development, and so contribute to achieving lifetime learning targets.
- Help unemployed people and those at a disadvantage in the jobs market to get back to work and to develop their abilities to the full.
- Stimulate the provision of high quality and flexible education and training, in support of the National Targets.

■ Encourage enterprise throughout the economy, particularly through the continued growth of small business and self-employment.

In Training and Enterprise, Priorities for Action (Training Agency, 1989), the Aims and Priorities for TECs were detailed:

■ to help businesses improve their performance by encouraging them to plan and undertake training to achieve clear business aims
■ to help ensure that young people acquire the skills the economy needs
■ to help ensure that unemployed people, and particularly the long-term unemployed, acquire the skills, experience and enterprise to help them find and keep a job
■ to encourage new businesses to start and existing businesses to grow
■ to help make the providers of vocational education aware of local labour market needs and to promote links between education and employers
■ to improve the training system by ensuring that there is an effective local, sectoral and national framework.

These aims and priorities related to the first TECs, to Industry Training Organisations, to Local Enterprise Agencies and to the Employment Department Training Agency. Underpinning all aims and priorities was a commitment to continue to promote equal access to training and enterprise for people at a disadvantage in the labour market.

NATIONAL EDUCATION AND TRAINING TARGETS

Foundation learning

■ By 1997, 80% of young people to reach NVQ Level II or equivalent.
■ Training and education to NVQ Level III (or equivalent) available to all young people who can benefit.
■ By 2000, 50% of young people to reach NVQ Level III (or equivalent).
■ Education and training provision to develop self-reliance, flexibility and breadth.

Lifetime learning

■ By 1996, all employees should take part in training or development activities as the norm.

■ By 1996, at least half of the employed workforce should be aiming for qualifications or units towards them within the NVQ, preferably in the context of individual action plans and with support from employers.

■ By 2000, 50% of the employed workforce should be qualified to NVQ or its academic equivalent as a minimum.

■ By 1996, at least half of the medium sized and larger organisations should qualify as Investors in People, assessed by the relevant TEC.

Specific details of initiatives such as Investors in People can be found in other sections of this book.

HOW DO TECs OPERATE?

There are now 82 TECs/LECs. The geographic areas covered by individual TECs vary. Each TEC, during its development phase, prepared a Corporate Plan to provide a basis for its operations. These plans also included information about the geographical area to be covered as well as the extent of support from the local community and priorities for change and improvement in the local labour market.

Each TEC Corporate Plan uses a market assessment as its basis – this includes a review of long and short term needs of businesses and individuals. The Plan includes a mission statement, three year strategic objectives, a framework for action, a business plan and an operational structure.

As always, the operation of TECs must have control arrangements which strike the right balance between local autonomy for TECs and central accountability for public funds. A total of £1.4 billion was spent on Department of Employment funded training, enterprise and education programmes during 1991/2 whilst the network of TECs was developing – the network of 82 TECs was completed in October 1991. The first TECs/LECs to become operational were Calderdale/Kirklees, Hertfordshire and Thames Valley Enterprise, all beginning in April 1990. The London TECs were the last to be established, each covering a specific area of London, during August to October 1991.

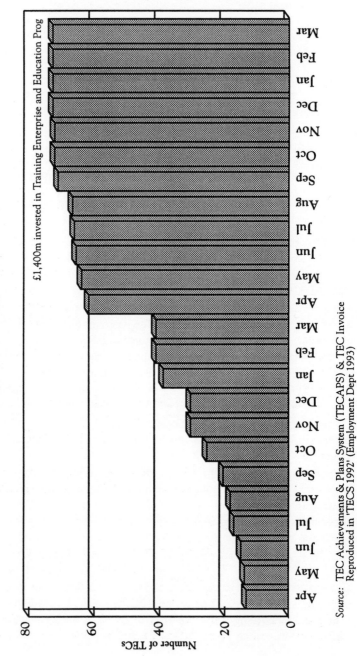

Growth of TEC Network

£1,400m invested in Training Enterprise and Education Prog

Number of TECs

Source: TEC Achievements & Plans System (TECAPS) & TEC Invoice
Reproduced in 'TECS 1992' (Employment Dept 1993)

TEC PERFORMANCE

Since the establishment of the TECs and LECs, greater importance has been placed on measurable outputs. During 1991/2, 25% of payments for the two biggest programmes (Youth Training and Employment Training) were based on achievements in terms of qualifications gained by trainees and job placements for Employment Training. This was an improvement on the 10% figure for 1990/91. It is estimated that the figure for 1993 will vary between 25% and 40%.

Performance related funding also exists for achievement in specified areas. Targets set for 1991/2 included:

- The number of people obtaining a National Vocational Qualification (NVQ) level II or above (level I for Special Training Needs Category B) and a job, self-employment or Enterprise Allowance Scheme (EAS) on leaving Youth Training.
- The number of long term unemployed people (2 years or more unemployed on entry) who have jobs, self employment or entered EAS three months after Employment Training.
- The number of YT and ET ethnic minority trainees who have jobs, self employed or entered EAS on leaving training (YT) or three months after training (ET).
- The number of trainees with disabilities on YT and ET securing jobs, self employment or entering EAS on leaving training (YT) or three months after leaving training (ET).
- The number of YT and ET trainees resident in special areas, or other appropriate group, who secure jobs, self employment or enter EAS on leaving training (YT) or three months after training (ET).

In 1991/2 performance related awards worth over £27 million were made to TECs where targets were achieved. For 1992, the priorities were stated as:

- ethnic minority trainees
- inner cities and special geographic areas
- trainees with disabilities
- Investors in People commitments
- education developments.

TECs and LECs have been involved in a number of national initiatives since their inception. These include Gateways, Access to Assessment,

Skillchoice, Investors in People and, of course, NVQs. All of these initiatives have attempted to support a particular aspect of change.

With each new initiative, TECs are provided with a 'Consultative Document' and then a 'Prospectus'. TECs, as independent companies, decide whether to bid for the funding available to take forward these initiatives; thus different TECs will be operating different initiatives at different times. For example, the Access to Assessment initiative is, in 1993, in its third year, whilst Skillchoice only began in April of that year.

There is a growing awareness that TECs need to integrate the various services and products they offer, and to provide more of a business focus with an understanding of business needs. Much attention has been given to the individual, with marketing and promotion directed through TEC networks of 'providers' – still mainly colleges. However, the greater emphasis on performance targets, with funding being linked to the achievement of greater numbers achieving qualifications (see National Targets and Performance above), has led to an acknowledgement that marketing to employers will yield better and faster results.

Perhaps this is also a recognition that a qualification, or part of a qualification, for work will only be of real value to any individual when it is also valued by the employer whom they hope it will impress?

─── 10 ───

Making the Most of the New Standards

10.1 INTRODUCTION

This chapter looks briefly at ways in which new competence-based standards can be used as a basis for a range of organisational planning and monitoring functions. Rather than presenting an ideal model it raises questions and suggests issues which need to be addressed. Indeed, there can be no ideal model – one of the basic concepts underlying the new forms of competence-based standards is their potential for *flexibility*. To suggest a model for their use would therefore be counter-productive.

If you keep in mind the key points – standards are *outcome-based* and assessment is about collecting *evidence of actual performance* – then you will be able to apply the real potential of competence-based approaches to your own organisational needs. Expansion of the ideas expressed here can be found in Fletcher, 1993.

10.2 STANDARDS AND ORGANISATIONAL DEVELOPMENT

Implementing a new form of standards which are explicit and measurable gives you the chance to consider and formalise market information and assess how you can capitalise on the opportunities (and minimise constraints) in current and future market scenarios.

Market opportunities in which implementation of standards can probably be most beneficial include:

- need for consistency in quality
- growth in the industry or sector
- introduction of new legislation
- introduction of technological change
- deregulation and competition
- raising of public image of the organisation.

Constraints on the introduction of standards include:

- lack of resources
- complexity and size of the task
- lack of management support
- fragmented sector (which delays standards development anyway).

When planning the evaluation of the introduction of competence-based standards and NVQs in relation to organisation development, the following checklist may be useful:

- What were the key objectives in implementing standards?
- What were the priority objectives?
- What were the objectives in each occupational area?
- What milestones to achievement of objectives have been identified?
- What are the resource implications?
- What actions have had the most impact on acceptance of standards within the company?
- What actions/issues have had the most impact on rejection of standards within the company?

10.3 EXPANDING THE USE OF STANDARDS

Once standards are in place for assessment of workplace performance, and for achievement of NVQs, you will be ready to consider their use in other areas of organisational activity.

Your choice of activities, and their priority ordering, will depend very much upon your current organisational structure, and the administrative, managerial and communication systems currently in place.

Standards may be used effectively in the following areas:

- performance appraisal
- manpower planning
- selection and recruitment

- multiskilling
- revision of job descriptions/functions
- training and development.

The last of these is considered in Chapter 12.

Standards can also be updated to incorporate changes within the organisation, including the introduction of new technology or reorganisation.

10.4 AN ACTION PLAN

When considering how to expand the use of standards within your organisation, you will need to establish a clear action plan.

Key questions you may consider will include:

- What needs to be done to achieve the introduction of standards for every employee within the organisation?
- Who is going to be responsible for implementation activities?
- In which key areas will we utilise standards (see list above)?
- How long will it take?
- How much will it cost?
- What are our priorities?
- How will we measure progress?

Your action plan may be structured as follows:

- purpose of document
- key objectives, priorities, actions, issues
- personnel resources and management structure
- finances
- standards in use (percentage of workforce)
- standards under development
- timescale
- evaluation
- implementation plan in each area of development.

10.5 STANDARDS AND PERFORMANCE APPRAISAL

If you are already using standards in continuous assessment of workplace performance (ie within NVQs), the expansion to a performance appraisal system will not be too difficult.

You may treat the ongoing assessment as 'formative' evidence and link this to the annual performance appraisal. There are one or two points to bear in mind in this connection, however.

First, you should avoid making the annual performance appraisal a 'summative' assessment which leads directly to award of NVQs or the units which constitute them. This would encourage a 'time-serving' basis for awards which runs counter to the aims of NVQs – individuals should have access to awards on the basis of their individual performance.

Second, you must consider how such systems will be perceived by those who use them. Assessment for NVQs is directly linked to an incentive/reward system – external recognition through qualification. Performance appraisal is often linked to promotion or merit bonus or salary structure.

You need to be clear how you plan to link the two kinds of assessment. If people achieve NVQs, does this lead automatically to promotion, or salary increase, or merit bonus? What will be the key purpose of the performance appraisal system? Is it a completely 'open' reporting system? Are 'promotion markings' or any part of the report kept secret from the individual? (It is to be hoped that most systems have moved on from this practice.)

When considering the use of competence-based standards in performance appraisal, therefore, you must also consider how your appraisal system links with ongoing assessment of workplace performance and also with any other incentive or reward systems which you currently (or are planning to) operate.

Establishing the performance appraisal system, once your objectives are clear, involves a process of utilising the competence-based standards in a format which will facilitate an annual feedback and review.

If assessment has been continuous throughout the year, then feedback at an appointed annual time should not come as any surprise. The appraisal interview will present a good opportunity for training needs to be clearly identified and agreed, together with a development plan, as well as establishing objectives for the next year. The explicit nature of competence-based standards will provide a sound basis for discussion, as will the requirement for evidence of performance. In short, the nature and purpose of performance appraisal need not change, but the basis for discussion can be more explicit and based on clearer forms of evidence of the past year's performance.

Figure 10.1, taken from Gerald Randell's *Staff Appraisal* (Randell, 1984), may be a helpful guide in considering the *functions* of performance appraisal in your organisation. Once you are clear on the specific functions that are applicable to your existing, or planned, scheme you can consider how best to utilise competence-based standards in this area.

10.6 STANDARDS AND MANPOWER PLANNING

Manpower planning is the systematic analysis of the company's resources, the construction of a forecast of its future manpower requirements from this base, with special concentration on the efficient use of manpower at both these stages, and the planning necessary to ensure that the manpower supply will match the forecast requirement (Bell, 1974).

Put more simply is: *manpower planning is ensuring that the right number of people are in the right place at the right time.*

When looking forward for your manpower needs, what current measures do you use? How clear are your future plans? How much do you know about the roles that people carry out in your organisation and the actual skills they need; or what new skills will be needed to cope with planned change?

These have always been the difficult questions faced by those responsible for considering the future needs of an organisation. Manpower planning has become a complex and sophisticated activity with computer models and complex mathematical techniques being used in forecasting. Competence-based standards are not going to solve these problems, but because of their explicit nature they can contribute to the more effective identification of skills and knowledge required in new work roles.

Manpower planning is really a series of activities:

■ analysis of current resources
■ forecasting of future needs
■ planning to supply these needs.

The activities of analysing current resources and forecasting future needs relate directly to the performance required. In turn, the performance required relates directly to the skills and knowledge expected of employees.

The purposes of an appraisal scheme are:

— to assess future potential
— to assess training and development needs
— to assess past performance
— to establish control of behaviour
— to bring about changes in behaviour
— to help improve current performance.

The main steps of exercising management control are:

— setting standards
— monitoring performance
— comparing performance with the standard
— taking action that may be needed (either to improve the performance or to change the standards).

The main intentions of an appraisal scheme are:

— *Evaluation*, to enable the organisation to share out money, promotions and perquisites (perks) apparently fairly
— *Auditing*, to discover the work potential, both present and future, of individuals and departments
— *Constructing succession plans* for manpower, departmental and corporate planning
— *Discovering training needs* by exposing inadequacies and deficiencies which could be remedied by training
— *Motivating staff* to reach organisational standards and objectives
— *Developing individuals* by advice, information and attempts at shaping their behaviour by praise or punishment
— *Checking the effectiveness* of personnel procedures and practices.

Figure 10.1 The functions of performance appraisal

Source: Gerald Randell, *Staff Appraisal*, Institute of Personnel Management

If performance in monitored on a continuous basis, and the results of this performance measurement collated as part of your evaluation exercise, you will have valuable data to inform your future plans.

10.7 STANDARDS, SELECTION AND RECRUITMENT

This section also incorporates the use of standards in the revision of job descriptions and functions.

Recruitment and selection is about choosing staff. Again this involves a number of activities:

Deciding what → Casting the → Shortlisting → Decision-
the job needs recruitment making
net

Staff selection may often be a process conducted by gut feeling, despite training of managers and personnel staff in a wide range of techniques. The use of clearly defined standards can help to develop this gut feeling approach into a more informed and informative one, for both the interviewer and the interviewee.

Let's take the first activity – deciding *what the job needs*.

If competence-based standards have been introduced, then the expectations of the job someone undertakes will be clearly defined in terms of standards or expectations of performance. These standards will include the skills and knowledge required, and a specified range of activities in which performance must be undertaken.

This then, will provide the basis on which a job specification and person specification can be devised.

In *casting the recruitment net* you may wish to consider which competence-based qualifications would provide evidence of the performance level you are seeking. In particular, there may be specific units of competence which make up the specification you have developed.

You can consider whether you need someone who has attained all the relevant units, or whether you are prepared to take someone who has *some* of them, requiring you to arrange training in those remaining.

This consideration of NVQs held by prospective candidates may be a consideration more for the future – NVQs are as yet fairly new and it will take some time for their full use in the labour market to be established. However, the exercise of planning by units of competence does help to focus your mind, and the minds of the prospective employees, on the issue of evidence of performance. This approach will contribute to your shortlisting and decision-making exercises. What evidence can candidates supply of their current level of expertise? How valid is that evidence?

You may even want to consider establishing an initial assessment for interviewees, or asking them to present what they feel is valid evidence of their current level of performance.

Don't forget also that the National Record of Vocational Achievement (NROVA, see p 56) is in itself a type of portfolio of evidence. Some certificates contained within it may be more of the traditional type, and some (especially for young people) may have been obtained on particular work experience or national training programmes, but it is a useful source of information.

10.8 STANDARDS AND MULTISKILLING

Because the process of 'multiskilling' involves looking at the transferability of skills and the relationship between various activities within an organisational structure, competence-based standards are of particular help in this area.

You will recall from Part I that competence-based standards are derived through a process of *functional* analysis. A focus on functions rather than tasks contributes to a broader view of competence and incorporates aspects of task and contingency management as well as operating within the working environment.

This functional basis of standards can be used to facilitate your analysis and planning of multiskilling activities. Industry Lead Bodies may even be able to supply you with details of the original functional analysis which led to the derivation of competence-based standards. Alternatively, a good external consultant who has worked on competence-based developments will be able to assist you.

An overview of the sectoral standards, particularly at the higher levels of 'key work roles' (from which units of competence are derived) will also give you valuable information.

The following Case Study outlines work of the UK Learning Organisations Network – a group of UK companies who have been working together to define competencies for change agents. Note the use of the word *competencies* and not *competences* – the latter being the UK (NVQ) style of competence-based standard.

The Case Study gives readers a look at alternative approaches to the development and introduction of a competence-based approach.

It focuses on one role within organisations and has yet to approach the difficult problem of rigour of assessment, but clearly demonstrates how a definitive link between a competence-based system and business needs is a key requirement for any organisation.

■ CASE STUDY ■

Change Agent Competencies
UK Learning Organisations Network*

The following Case Study, kindly provided by Time Manager International, shows how a set of change agent competencies has been developed by member organisations of the UK Learning Organisation Network. The case study also illustrates three issues:

■ an initial networking process where generic competencies can be devised to suite the strategic human resource requirements of a broad range of commercial and non-commercial organisations
■ how competence development can be driven by practical business requirements
■ that competence development can be relatively inexpensive if driven by partner organisations which have a clear vision of what they are trying to achieve.

The Learning Organisation Network

The Learning Organisation Network is an informal group of private and public sector organisations which have demonstrated their commitment to the concept of the Learning Organisation. Member organisations include Rover, Digital Equipment, Midland Bank, Sainsburys, Time Manager International, Lucas, Rank Xerox, Milton Keynes College, the NHS and Royal Mail.

The Group first met in London in November 1992, following an initiative from Rover, Digital Equipment and the RSA with support from the HRD Partnership. A second meeting was held in April 1993 at Rover where Barrie Oxtoby from the Rover Learning Business shared the work that Rover had done in developing a range of change agent competencies. Members of the Group saw the value of this work and a team, co-ordinated by Ron Dillon, then Training Quality Assurance Manager at Rank Xerox, was formed to take it further.

The Vision

The vision of the Network at this time was to devise a set of change agent competencies that:

---

* Written and compiled by Gary Ling of Time Manager International.

- were relevant, credible and conceptually sound
- were sufficiently flexible to support the specific requirements of individual member companies
- recognised what people had already done
- potentially formed the basis of future development activity
- facilitated a self-assessment process that could be effectively and speedily validated
- allowed people who do not see themselves as change agents to recognise that they are.

Once the competencies had been developed, the role of the network was envisaged as being similar to that of an awarding body. In a less structured way, than, for example, the awarding of NVQs, members nominated individuals within their organisations who they assessed as being change agents. In recognition of this, these individuals were then awarded certificates carrying the names and logos of all participating organisations.

Clearly, this vision was novel in its approach to the development of competencies. One team member described the way in which member organisations, within the Learning Organisation Network, would work together in this process as a 'kind of change agent keiretsu'. It required the commitment of all concerned to the integrity of the process but since the essence of the change agent competencies is a recognition of continual individual and *'organisational'* learning, this was in keeping with the aims and objectives of the Learning Organisation Network.

The Process

Rather than start with a blank sheet of paper, the team at the Rover Learning Business carried out an initial trawl of existing development work in the area of change management, before they embarked on devising their own set of change agent competencies. They contacted several professional bodies but found that the competency work currently underway appeared to be developed by 'systems professionals and lawyers who had little feeling for people'.

As a result, over a three month period, the Rover Learning Business started work on its own set of change agent competencies for leaders within the Rover organisation, which were linked closely to supporting the company's business strategy. The key question addressed by this work was: 'What competencies do you need to

make the learning process work from a learning business viewpoint?'
Initially, 82 competencies were developed in this way and tested
internally with change agents within Rover.

In networking with other organisations interested in developments
in this area, Rover came across the work of Peritas, the ICL company
specialising in people and organisational development. Peritas had
developed a practical approach to competencies that they were
marketing externally as a commercial enterprise. It was the initial
contributions of both these organisations that the team from the
Learning Organisation Network set to work on and Peritas has now
used the Rover Framework to produce a model of change and change
agent competencies for any business manager. The Learning
Organisation Network is now validating these competencies in a variety of business environments.

The Framework

The *'change cycle'* at Fig. 10.2 outlines the model of change within
which Peritas have developed this set of change agent competencies.

The change cycle illustrates the stages that change agents have to
go through in order to bring about value–adding change. Changing
processes, organisational structure and the skills and attitudes of
people, are the three areas which are specifically identified as the
targets of change.

Clearly, change agents have to understand the external influences
that affect both **best practice** and their organisations' **business
needs**. While many businesses will be affected by the same external
influences, such as those which impact the economic environment
generally, change agents will also be expected to appreciate factors
that specifically impact their organisations.

From **best practice and business needs** the Learning Organisation Network team have developed a set of competencies for each
of the areas identified in the change cycle.

The Future

Although still in its infancy, the process by which these competencies
have been developed so far, has generated some considerable interest
in Europe, where at a recent meeting of the European Consortium
for Learning Organisations, the UK's work in this area was recognised
as being significantly further advanced that its continental partners. A

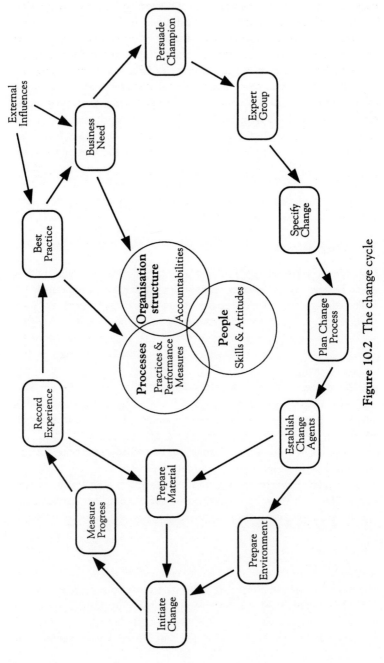

Figure 10.2 The change cycle

study group has now been set up in Finland to change and develop these competencies further.

Meanwhile, while recognising that these competencies are not cast in stone, organisations in the Learning Organisation Network are soon to be invited to make a more tangible commitment to the competencies developed so far, by offering the use of their corporate logos on the first certificates issued to those individuals recognised as competent change agents.

—11—

Making the Most of New Forms of Assessment

Within the new system of NVQs, assessment is a 'process of obtaining evidence and making judgements about that evidence'. More traditional forms of assessment require assessors both to determine the standards to be achieved and to assess evidence against those standards (as in a course-based programme of study). Within NVQs, the standards are already established and are in explicit (and written) format for both assessor and assessee. Assessment decisions therefore focus on whether the assessee has presented sufficient evidence of the right quality.

11.1 EVIDENCE OF COMPETENCE

Assessment of normal work performance offers the most natural form of evidence of competence. Where this is not possible, perhaps due to operational constraints or requirements of health and safety, workplace assessment can be supplemented by simulations, or by competency tests (like skills tests). In general, most observation of workplace assessment will need to be supplemented by at least oral questioning in order to determine evidence of transferability of skills and knowledge application across the specified range of work activity.

Evidence of performance can also be obtained during the course of a training programme when trainees practise and demonstrate skills and application of knowledge. In this way, assessment can be integrated with the learning process and provide useful feedback to trainees.

Given this performance-focused nature of new forms of assessment, how best can they be used to benefit your company?

11.2 PERFORMANCE APPRAISAL AND MANPOWER PLANNING

The previous chapter briefly outlined the use of competence-based standards within performance appraisal systems, and suggested that ongoing assessment may be treated as formative and thus contribute to the annual performance appraisal. It is worth noting again here, though, that you should avoid making the annual performance appraisal a 'summative' assessment which leads directly to the award of an NVQ. This would reinstate a time-based element to the achievement of NVQs, whereas one of their key benefits is individual access to awards based on individual performance.

Ongoing assessment, using competence-based systems, provides an up-to-date audit of individual and group performance. You might want to consider the best ways in which you can collate information to maintain your own records of improved performance.

As individuals are assessed, and achieve units of competence, you may wish to record this centrally to contribute to your manpower planning activities. This is also particularly relevant where you need to draw together project teams for particular assignments. You might consider the use of computerised systems for recording current skill levels; there are a variety available or under development which can be used for this purpose.

11.3 ASSESSMENT AND TRAINING

The design and delivery of training, using competence-based standards and assessment, is perhaps one of the most attractive benefits to individual companies. For this reason, Chapter 12 deals exclusively with this issue.

However, the issue of assessment in relation to training needs analysis and evaluation is also a key contributor to improvement of company performance.

11.4 TRAINING NEEDS ANALYSIS

Using explicit standards of performance, assessment of current levels of skill and knowledge, and identification of the 'training gap' are greatly facilitated. This process also ensures a common standard both for the initial assessment process, and for the targeted training which follows.

Trainers will need to be experienced in the use of competence-based standards and in their assessment. Line managers, if trained in work-based assessment, will be in an ideal position to identify training needs of both individuals and groups and pass this information on to the training department.

This somewhat changes the role of the trainer, but in line with current trends. The trainer becomes a key adviser and consultant in the company and provides support to line managers in both the needs-analysis and solution-finding role.

11.5 ACCREDITATION OF PRIOR LEARNING (APL)

Earlier chapters briefly outlined the APL concept and process. However, it is in the context of training needs analysis that APL becomes a truly valuable tool.

It is worth reiterating that APL is not an autonomous process, but an integral part of competence-based assessment. When operated in-company, or within an 'approved' assessment centre (see below), it requires trained assessors, and may involve additional verification costs. However, it is likely that the return on what is usually a minor investment in these areas will be well worth the commitment.

'APL is a process which enables the identification, assessment and certification of a person's vocationally relevant past achievements' (BTEC, 1990). One of the key purposes of APL at national level is to improve *access* to vocational qualifications. Many adults, for example, are reluctant to return to long periods of study in order to obtain a qualification when they feel they would simply be repeating learning in order to prove that they can do what they already do every day!

On an organisational (ie company) level, APL can offer a solution to this adult perception and be used as a motivational tool to encourage individual and group development. In addition, the company benefits by improved targeting of training – to say nothing of a more cost-effective use of the training budget.

We might think of APL as a kind of skills audit or training audit. It can also be an initial motivator for the introduction of competence-based standards and NVQs, offering credit towards NVQs for those who can successfully provide evidence of competence which matches the specified standards.

All the major awarding bodies now have policies and published guidelines regarding APL, and verification processes are being included across many occupational sectors.

If you are considering using APL, first review the hypothetical scenario which follows, then contact the relevant awarding bodies for the NVQs you plan to use to check that APL guidelines are in place.

The purpose of APL guidelines in each occupational area is twofold. First, they help assessors with information on the types of evidence which will be acceptable; and second, they provide help for external (ie awarding body) verifiers.

Let's consider a hypothetical scenario for introducing APL.

Company X introducing APL

Company X, which operates in the manufacturing sector, employs 5,000 people on a national basis. Occupations include those in the manufacturing process, administrative and management staff.

Relevant standards and NVQs have been identified and plans for their introduction are under consideration.

The company would like to use the competence-based assessment process to take a skills audit of its workforce and appreciates that the use of APL would facilitate this, providing a motivator for staff, and being an integral part of the planned change.

It explores the possibility of using APL with relevant awarding bodies and finds that policies and guidelines are in place. The requirements of operating APL include:

- assessors who are trained in the concepts and operation of APL
- verification arrangements agreed with awarding body.

The company had planned to train line managers and trainers in work-based assessment and explored the use of external consultants to undertake this work. They checked that the consultants were fully capable of delivering a training package which included APL concepts and techniques. They also checked that the consultants were approved by the appropriate awarding bodies. This enabled the company to link training and verification of assessors to award of qualifications in assessment, thus providing a further motivator for staff who had been designated to the assessment role.

Discussions with the awarding body regarding verification arrangements revealed that arrangements for external verifiers to visit the company could be negotiated on the basis of the number of assessors and candidates. A verifier would monitor the work of a number of assessors. The company would be required to pay a daily rate for each verification visit.

The company then considered its internal policy and operational arrangements and set up a management group to establish:

- a company policy on APL
- a named individual with overall responsibility for the introduction and operation of APL in-company
- a staff development programme.

The decision to pilot APL with the administrative staff in one region was taken. Appropriate staff were designated as assessors and were trained in both work-based assessment and APL, using published competence-based standards as the basis for assessment.

Administrative staff were provided with details of the pilot through an article in the company newsletter. Line managers were briefed at regular network meetings and then discussed the pilot with their staff during regular staff meetings. Volunteers were sought and identified.

Those staff selected for the pilot met with their designated assessor to draw up an assessment plan. This identified the units of competence for which individual staff felt they could provide sufficient evidence of current performance. A timescale for assessment was also agreed.

Individual staff had been made fully aware that the collection of evidence from past achievements was entirely their responsibility, as was the organisation of this evidence into a 'portfolio'. Each individual had a copy of the relevant standards of performance and would organise their portfolio to match the specified units and elements of competence.

The company allowed individuals time for the collection of evidence, arranged on an individual basis with line managers. Designated assessors (who were also line managers in some instances) provided ongoing support and advice during the evidence collection stage.

All designated assessors met on a regular basis to exchange ideas regarding progress and to provide a forum for assessor support. The APL manager (who had been established at policy-making level and had overall responsibility for the introduction and operation of APL) attended assessor meetings and also visited individual candidates to monitor and report on general progress.

When individual candidates had completed their portfolio, with guidance and support from their designated assessor, the assessor conducted a final review of evidence presented. If satisfied with the *validity, currency, authenticity* and *sufficiency* of the evidence, the assessor then made a recommendation for award of appropriate units.

The evidence was reviewed by an external verifier who either decided to support the claim for credit, or referred any discrepancies back to the assessor. The individual concerned was informed of any difficulties and given the opportunity to provide further evidence for reassessment.

Successful individuals were awarded the units for which sufficient and valid evidence had been presented. The awarding body issued 'credit notes' for each unit which could be retained by the individual. The company paid for the issue of these unit certificates at £6 per unit.

A final review of achievements led to mutual agreement of training needs and future development plans. These were recorded on the individual development plan and reported to the training department. The individual's training needs would therefore be recorded and appropriate training solutions planned.

11.6 INDIVIDUAL DEVELOPMENT PLANS

The introduction and use of individual development plans are worth consideration. As competence-based assessment is *individualised*, linking assessment to personal and career development becomes a simpler process to operate within the company.

Again, you will need to consider the supporting structure of development plans and career progression. You may need to modify your existing in-company schemes, particularly in the context of documentation and recording systems. You might also like to consider ways in which *self-assessment* can be incorporated into the ongoing development process.

Information from individual development plans could be collated to contribute to annual training strategies and detailed plans.

11.7 MEETING NVQ CRITERIA

Whether you use documentation and procedures available within the relevant NVQ structure, or you choose to devise your own, a key requirement is that the assessment scheme meets the criteria set by the NCVQ. These criteria are summarised in Part III.

The NVQ criteria relate to *quality of assessment* and *maintenance of national standards*. They also ensure that an *equal opportunities policy* is incorporated into working practice.

If you operate an in-company assessment scheme, you may want to link the development of your employees to in-company training programmes. This is acceptable as long as your in-company specifications for achievement of NVQs do not make completion of these training programmes mandatory.

Individuals may learn in a variety of ways, including through work experience. NVQs are awarded for *successful assessment of competence performance*, not for attendance on specified courses.

11.8 GETTING HELP

If you are considering ways in which you can make the best use of competence-based assessment, there are a number of sources of information and direct support.

Awarding bodies

These bodies will be able to provide information regarding assessment requirements for particular NVQs, and for APL. They also provide external verifiers and can advise you of the fees involved. Remember, some Industry Lead Bodies are also awarding bodies.

Colleges

Many colleges have now radically changed their provision and some operate as approved assessment centres. Check with your local college provider to see what services are available. These may include college assessors who can visit the company, APL, or assistance with development programmes. Make sure the college has trained assessors and the facilities to assess in relevant occupational areas.

Private providers

Some private training providers will be recommended by Industry Lead Bodies or approved by TECs and can help you with the development of standards, introduction of competence-based assessment,

APL, assessor training and so on. Make sure you choose a provider who has experience in the field of competence-based provision.

Accredited Training Centres

The majority of these centres, which offer training in relation to national training programmes (eg training credits and ET) are based in colleges. Their provision has recently expanded to include a more diverse range of training programmes. They can also assist with assessor training.

Whichever type of assistance you choose, it is best first to consider exactly what type of help you need within all areas of competence-based provision. It is usually advantageous to use a single source which can provide help across the board than to find you have to contract with two or three different organisations to achieve your total objectives.

Assessor/Verifier Awards

In 1993, national standards for assessors and verifiers were published. In addition, the publication of the Common Accord confirmed the requirement for accredited staff in NVQ centres (including employer premises). The following section provides information on the Assessor and Verifier Awards and how to achieve them.

✎ INFORMATION SECTION ✎

Assessor and Verifier Awards

In 1993, the Training and Development Lead Body (TDLB) approved units of competence for Assessors and Verifiers who operate within the NVQ system. These units received NCVQ approval and were launched for use by all assessors and verifiers.

In addition the Common Accord (see p 171) was published in the same year. This document confirmed that all assessors and verifiers for NVQs would be required to achieve the TDLB units (currently within 12 months of registration).

The Assessor and Verifier Units cover all roles involved in NVQ operation:

■ Unit D31 – designing assessment
■ Unit D32 – workplace assessor

- Unit D33 – assessing diverse evidence (eg portfolios, APL)
- Unit D34 – internal verifier
- Unit D35 – external verifier
- Unit D36 – APL adviser.

In line with NCVQ requirements, these units are achieved by **demonstration of competence in the role**. Thus, all assessors and verifiers must actually undertake the role in order to provide sufficient valid evidence of performance.

This creates something of a 'chicken and egg' situation for many people – you need the assessor awards to be accredited (or licensed in some cases), but you need to assess people in order to achieve the award!

The Common Accord document acknowledges this dilemma and arrangements now include a period of 12 months in which all practising assessors and verifiers can collect sufficient evidence for accreditation. During this time, their work will be monitored by an approved verifier.

The quality assurance system for NVQs (in ideal form) operates as follows.

- External verifier (employee of awarding body)
- Internal verifier (in-house at assessment centre, which can be an employer)
- Work place assessors (in-house at assessment centre)
- Candidates.

Employers can become approved centres for NVQs (although this is not always practical or cost effective for all NVQs or all companies). To do so, the employer must demonstrate that the above quality assurance framework can operate in-house, that assessors and verifiers are working towards accredited status and that the in-house assessment system meets national requirements.

This can get a bit unwieldy when a number of NVQs are being introduced, especially if each has its own assessment documentation and each is given by a different awarding body! For this reason, many companies make use of national standards (including those for assessors and verifiers) without introducing NVQs. However, by designing an in-house assessment system to cover all relevant occupational areas, a company can overcome these difficulties.

In-house assessors and verifiers must be trained (see page 102 for help in this area) – it is dangerous to assume that the use of a competence-based system can simply be 'picked up' – it requires an adjustment in thinking. A lack of adequate training can result in a poor quality operation – which will add nothing to the organisational or individual benefits of introduction.

Further information on the assessor and verifier awards can be obtained from the awarding bodies. Each awarding body has its own development and accreditation system (and related costs). Costs should include:

■ individual registration fee (check if this covers all units or only one)
■ certification fee (per unit)
■ licence fee (not applicable to all awarding bodies).

Check also whether the registration fee includes provision of materials for use by assessors – log books, assessment records etc – and whether these are mandatory.

The awarding bodies also approve centres to offer the assessor and verifier awards. This will include provision of training, assessment and recommendation for certification. Check carefully on costs involved which could include:

■ training of assessors/verifiers
■ adviser support
■ work place assessment
■ telephone support
■ portfolio assessment
■ individual interview following portfolio assessment
■ recommendation for certification
■ awarding body registration fee
■ awarding body materials
■ certification fee.

Make sure you get value for money as well as quality of delivery and support!

You can obtain full lists of approved centres from the awarding bodies.

There are also various open learning programmes on the market and an assessor development pack is available from NCVQ.

—12—

Competence-based Training

As we noted in earlier chapters, the flexibility provided by competence-based systems is one of the key attractions for employers. With explicit standards of performance to use as a base, and tools such as accreditation of prior learning (APL) to both facilitate training needs analysis and motivate employees, the attraction is clear.

However, if training is to be effective, both in terms of improving performance and in relation to costs, then trainers must understand the key concepts and issues involved in the development of competence-based standards.

Trainers with responsibility for the design of programmes need to understand how standards are developed. This is outlined briefly in Part I, but a synopsis of development methodology is given here as a reference point.

12.1 STANDARDS DEVELOPMENT

Competence-based standards are *employment-led*. This means they are developed *by* the industry, *for* the industry. They therefore reflect the expectations of employment.

Standards are developed at *sector level* and through a process of *functional analysis*. This involves beginning with the *key purpose* of the sectoral occupation and identifying the *key functions* undertaken.

The concept of functions is highly important. Many earlier analysis techniques focused on tasks, which represent a lower level of activity. The following may be helpful in distinguishing between these different terms:

Tasks – activities undertaken at work

Functions – the purpose of activities undertaken at work.

This is a very broad-brush distinction, but it recognises the need to identify *outcomes* of activity when deriving occupational standards of competence. By asking why an activity is undertaken, one is establishing the purpose of the activity, which leads to the outcome or result of that activity.

Identifying outcomes maintains a focus on *performance*. Competence-based standards, as noted above, must reflect expectations of workplace performance.

Once the outcomes have been identified, and established as either *units of competence* or as *elements of competence* (see below), the next question is 'What are the qualities of these outcomes that indicate competent performance?'

The terms *units* and *elements of competence* were explained in Part 1 (Chapter 3). As a brief reminder, a *unit of competence* represents work activity which:

■ can be undertaken by one individual

■ is worthy of separate certification (ie as a 'credit' towards a full NVQ).

An *element of competence* is:

■ a description of something which a person who works in a given occupational area should be able to do. It reflects action, behaviour or outcomes which have real meaning in the occupational sector to which it relates.

When we ask 'what are the qualities of these outcomes', therefore, we are seeking the *criteria* by which an assessor can judge whether an individual's performance meets the required standard. The results of our research into qualities, therefore, provide us with *performance criteria*. These reflect the critical aspects of performance – all those qualities which are essential to competent performance.

A final stage of deriving standards refers to the range of contexts, conditions or contingencies in which a competent person must operate. These are researched and incorporated into a *range statement*.

Some standards defined by Industry Lead Bodies may also include statements relating to *evidence*. This is a guideline for assessors providing information on the type or range of evidence – both performance evidence and knowledge evidence – required.

One question often asked is 'If competence-based standards focus on performance, what about the *knowledge* that people need to do their job competently?' A basic concept underlying the development of competence-based standards is that application of knowledge is an integrated part of competent performance. This means two things:

■   it is application of knowledge and not knowledge itself that is important to competent performance
■   application of knowledge can be assessed through assessment of competence performance.

Some knowledge will be *implicit* in assessment of performance. For example, if an individual performs competently (ie to specified standards) on a similar activity, but in a different context, then an assessor may, with reasonable safety, assume that that individual has successfully applied knowledge of similar, but not identical, working requirements to the second situation.

In some situations, assessors may need to collect evidence of relevant application of knowledge through *oral questioning*.

It may not be possible to observe an individual performing in the complete range of workplace activities, or to assess the full amount of knowledge required, simply by observation of performance. In this instance, other forms of assessment may be used. These may include simulation, oral questioning, skills test or assignment.

Readers can supplement this very brief outline of standards development methodology by reading Part I. Further technical information can be found in the documents provided by TEED (which are listed in the Reference Section of Part III).

12.2 STANDARDS, NVQs AND TRAINING PROGRAMMES

One important point, made several times in Part I, is that NVQs have *nothing whatsoever to do with training programmes*. This addresses the common misconception that units of competence are training modules. This is far from correct.

A unit of competence is a unit of *assessment* and *certification*. The standards (elements, performance criteria and range statements) incorporated within a unit of competence, specify the *performance* required in the workplace.

Units of competence are *outcome-based*
Training modules are *input-based.*

Training modules are designed to provide the development (or input) that individuals and groups need in order to achieve and maintain the required standards. They may contain practical exercises and assignments, but these represent practice rather than actual performance in the main.

Assessment of practical work on a training programme should be to the same standards as those used in the workplace. Evidence of performance in these practical exercises can *contribute towards* final achievement of the relevant unit, but should not serve as a 'one-off' or any form of 'single judgement'.

The issue of *standards development* and the distinction between *units of competence* and *training modules* is critical to succesful training design. You should make sure you are clear on these issues if you are planning the design of competence-based training.

12.3 DESIGNING COMPETENCE-BASED TRAINING

Experience with a wide range of trainers indicates that the key difficulty they experience in the design of competence-based training is the switch in thinking required to think in *outcome* terms.

Any trainer experienced in the design of training programmes automatically thinks in terms of training objectives and content. Competence-based training still has objectives and still has a clear content. The essential difference is that explicit, *outcome-based* standards are used as the basis of design.

Once trainers have grasped the concepts involved, the actual task of design is far less daunting. As with all competence-based activities, the design starts with standards.

The trainer should review the standards relevant to the work role of the target audience and ask the following questions:

- What do people actually have to *do?*
- What underpinning knowledge and skill do they need?
- What training activities would best suit
  - the target audience?
  - the contribution of training to achievement of standards?
  - the constraints of time, cost, location?

■ What assessment activities can be built in to the training programme?
■ How can the training be evaluated?

You will notice that these questions are not too far removed from current practice. Standards, and the components of standards, are more explicit, facilitating the use of assessment activities within the training programme, and thus providing ideal opportunities for self-, peer and trainer assessment.

If trainers focus on the key concepts outlined above and on the key questions to be applied to the design of training, they will have made a good start on introducing competence-based training within the company. Further help is available in Fletcher, 1992a.

12.4 TRAINING EVALUATION

If you build assessment activities into your training programmes, you are already contributing to an effective evaluation of the training itself, as well as providing motivation and feedback for your participants.

You should also plan a longer-term evaluation in advance, again using competence-based standards as a foundation for this planning.

As the standards specify both what individuals must do and how well they must do it (in the workplace), the standards themselves provide the *workplace performance measures*.

To conduct a realistic evaluation of training effectiveness, you will first need to take a measure of current performance. If your company has introduced accreditation of prior learning (see p 134), information on this initial measurement of current performance will be available. If not, you might consider ways in which you can collect it.

If you are familiar with the concept of evidence of competence – particularly if you have been trained in workplace assessment – you will be able to plan this initial measuring of performance as a process of evidence collection. The nature and type of evidence will depend on the context, the operational requirements and the time constraints involved.

A brief measurement of current performance could be established through a pre-course questionnaire, or pre-course exercise. This would give you a starting point, but would obviously not be as effective as a more detailed assessment. Pre-course documentation should be provided to both target audience and their line managers. If you obtain an assessment (independently) from both, you will be able to make some comparison of results.

Your pre-course documentation should be carefully planned, and should include the specific standards used in designing the training programme.

Post-course evaluation then follows a similar pattern. The key purpose of training is to improve performance; your evaluation should therefore aim to identify clear improvement in performance.

If you have close liaison with the section heads and line managers, you could set up a short-term assessment system to contribute to your evaluation exercise. However, if your company has introduced NVQs, line managers should be assessing competence on a regular basis, and recording the results (evidence) of assessment – so you will have a ready-made assessment system. If your company has also introduced individual development plans (see p 137), then most of your work has been done already!

12.5 USING EXTERNAL PROVIDERS

If you don't design your own in-company training, or if you use external providers for some training design and delivery, the same rules apply. However, as has been mentioned several times already, make sure you choose a provider who has experience in competence-based developments, and particularly one who understands the concepts and issues involved.

12.6 GAINING EXTERNAL RECOGNITION FOR IN-COMPANY TRAINING

Another question often asked, and which illustrates yet another misconception about new competence-based developments, is 'How can we get our training accredited by the NCVQ?' If you have grasped the key concepts outlined within this book, you will know that the answer to this is that you can't.

The NCVQ does not accredit training programmes. NVQs are comprised of units of assessment and can only be achieved by successful *assessment of workplace performance*.

Should your company wish to gain recognition for its in-company training, however, this can be achieved. The recognition of training usually takes one of two forms: credit exemption and advanced standing.

Credit exemption and advanced standing can be negotiated with educational institutions. A formal agreement (with a provider of a specific programme of study) is established. This allows individuals to be 'exempt from' or to be 'credited with' certain parts of that programme. It is the relationship to a specific programme of study which distinguishes this form of credit from that involved in the APL process. NVQs are not linked to any one programme of study. Units within an NVQ are units of assessment (not training units). Awards of NVQs therefore denote workplace performance achievement, not learning achievement.

With NVQs:

- assessment of performance (competence-based) is individualised
- assessment of performance (competence-based) can lead to award of national vocational qualifications.

External recognition of (in-company) training programmes refers to (approval of) the actual content, duration, delivery etc of the learning programme itself. Anyone who completes the (approved) learning programme can gain 'credit exemption' or 'advanced standing' for a specified course of study.

One of the most widely known systems of this type was the CATS scheme (credit accumulation and transfer). This was operated by the CNAA (Council for National Academic Awards) and offered a system whereby credits obtained through approved learning programmes could be counted towards a first degree – even if those credits were obtained in different places and at different times.

This system of 'credit rating' is useful if your workforce usually aim for degrees or professional qualifications – but you should remember that higher-level qualifications are also being revised to a competence-based format.

The developments undertaken by the Management Charter Initiative (MCI) under the direction of the National Forum for Management Education and Development (NFMED) have created much interest, particularly in the last year as draft competences for managers have emerged.

The following, and final, case study provides information on MCI's Experienced Manager APL Project and offers valuable information for all companies considering the introduction of the accreditation of prior learning (APL) process and/or the use of management competences. The results of this project are now in use as the 'Crediting Competence' system of Approved Centres. Contact MCI for details.

■ CASE STUDY ■

Accreditation of Prior Learning for Experienced Managers

The Management Charter Initiative (MCI), the Industry Lead Body for development of national standards of competence for managers, embarked on a major APL pilot project in September 1989, funded by the Training Agency. The project seeks to:

- develop a credible and rigorous APL methodology for experienced managers
- pilot-test it with academic and non-academic centres including employers
- develop a national implementation strategy.

The proposal for the project came from the Experienced Managers Working Party, set up under the chairmanship of Paul Jervis of the Bristol Business School. This working party, established in late 1988 to address the development needs of experienced managers, reports to the Standards Development Committee of the National Forum for Management Education and Development, MCI's parent body.

There are now 13 pilot centres participating, ranging from training providers and colleges in England and Scotland to MCI networks and employers. British Rail, British Gas and the British Institute of Management are all directly involved. All centres have sought accreditation from either BTEC, Scotvec or the CNAA for certificate qualifications (the MCI is currently working with these and other awarding bodies to develop NVQs and SVQs based on its national competence standards).

HOW DOES APL WORK?

APL focuses directly on the national standards of management competence developed by the MCI. These are incorporated into a workbook designed specifically for managers.

APL involves managers reflecting on their own experience, analysing competences gained against units of national standards and developing a portfolio of evidence to demonstrate that competence. Each unit represents a credit towards a qualification, ultimately an NVQ in management.

The kinds of evidence managers are bringing forward include minutes and action points of meetings, letters and memos, business plans, appraisal forms and certificates of training. In addition, managers support their evidence with their own personal accounts of performance, reflecting on what they did and why.

Figure 12.1 shows how the MCI's model works.

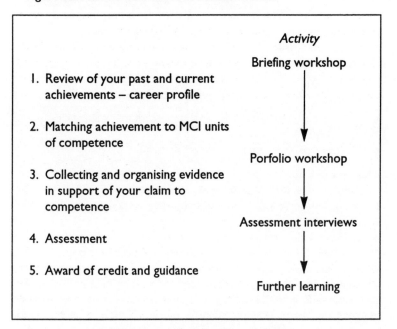

Figure 12.1 The MCI model of APL

Group work is a particular feature of the process. Managers attend workshops and in most centres form peer groups to review experience and evidence.

In each centre, there are trained assessors as well as APL advisors who guide managers through the process.

There is much enthusiasm for APL among participants

Perhaps the most important and encouraging finding is that the APL process works. Candidates have been able to produce portfolios that can be used to assess their competence. Participants in the process are enthusiastic about their involvement with APL. There is clear evidence that APL will be a popular route with experienced managers.

APL is a broader process than we originally thought

In the context of our original definition of the problem of experienced managers, APL was seen as a useful tool that would be used within some form of management development activity.

It was envisaged that APL (or some other technique) would be used to identify where experienced managers were competent (and thus where they were not) as a precursor to a development activity aimed at filling the competence gaps so identified.

Experience to date indicates that this model underestimates the value of the APL process itself as a vehicle for personal development. We now believe that there is considerable developmental value in the APL process itself (at least as it has been designed and operated in the project).

APL does not have to be restricted to 'experienced managers'

Although the work on APL of managerial competence has been developed in the context of a working party looking at the management development needs of 'experienced managers' as defined above, we can now see that the process can be used more widely. It is not only relevant to 'experienced managers' – it is a portfolio approach to management development and could be used as the assessment vehicle for a structured learning programme.

The APL process is not suitable for everybody

Perhaps as a counter to the above, there is evidence that not everyone is suited to the APL process. The reasons why some find more problems with APL than others seem more likely to lie in issues of personality, personal characteristics and style than in factors connected with education, work experience or job.

We think it is important, particularly if APL is to be offered widely in future, that more work is done to identify those for whom APL may be less successful.

One indication to emerge from our work so far is that, since APL is a self-managed process, it needs people who are self-reliant. It may be possible to identify other characteristics necessary to cope with the APL process, or to indicate in more detail the support structure that might be necessary to prevent problems arising.

APL is not easy, nor is it cheap, and there can be a high drop-out rate

An indicator of the demanding nature of APL is that there can be a high drop-out rate. Our experience shows that it is very important to get participants' expectations right at the outset. They must not expect the process to be 'quick and dirty' and they must recognise the need, and be prepared, to put in a considerable amount of effort themselves.

We noted with interest that the pilot centres charging the most for the APL process had the lowest drop-out rates. In part, this is to be expected. If people are paying large sums of money, they are likely to persist to ensure that they do get value from their investment. But this may also indicate that the centres concerned have managed, by making the process appear expensive, to indicate to participants at the outset the scale of the commitment they need to make.

Another factor that may influence drop-out rates is the degree of support participants received from the centres at which they are registered. The evaluation of the project when finished will need to investigate whether there are any clear links between completion rates and levels of support provided.

At this stage, it is difficult to put a cost on the typical APL process for experienced managers. However, it is becoming clear that APL is not a low-cost way of obtaining management qualifications. It is likely that when detailed cost estimates are available, APL will be seen as an effective and high-quality way of proving managerial competence rather than a cheap alternative to conventional 'training'.

APL is not easy for the unwaged

Initial indications are that APL, when related to management competences, is not easy for those not currently in employment. The main reason for this appears to be the accessibility of 'evidence' needed to demonstrate competence. Even if participants have reached the required level of competence in former employment, if they are no longer with the relevant employers they can face difficulties in collecting a sufficient portfolio of evidence.

The 'ownership' of the APL process is a key factor

The pilot projects have included those based on employers, on polytechnics and colleges, on management development and training organisations, and on professional bodies. This will enable the evaluation to determine whether any one form of organisation and management of the APL process is better than any other.

Preliminary indications are that the employer-based models may offer a number of advantages. However, if this does prove to be true, it will raise other questions about the best form of partnership between employers and training providers.

MCI Crediting Competence centres

From early 1991, the MCI established new centres, including its own networks, to deliver APL under the MCI's name. The MCI took on the central promotional role, keeping a register of centres and trained assessors and providing marketing facilities. The MCI also offers APL directly to employers.

The APL product consists of:

- workbook for experienced managers
- guidelines for APL assessors
- guidelines for APL advisors
- manual for APL centres
- training for APL assessors and advisors.

(Further information can be gained from the MCI (see page 236).

12.7 SUMMARY

This revised edition has attempted to combine an understanding of key concepts with a practical application of new developments in competence-based provision. It provides details of latest developments including new initiatives and financial support for employers and individuals.

I trust that the text, together with its checklists and the various perspectives provided by the case studies have served to give you a clearer insight into these developments, helped you to avoid some of the pitfalls, and provided you with some tools for active decision-making and hands-on experience.

In Part III, you will find references, addresses and other useful material as a resource for helping you through your company's change programme.

Part Three

Help Menu: Information, Addresses and References for Practitioners

Quick Reference Guide

National Vocational Qualifications – Criteria for Accreditation*

This chapter sets out the criteria used by the NCVQ to decide whether or not a qualification can be accepted as part of the national framework of vocational qualifications.

The criteria are stated without detailed explanation or examples; those interested in submitting qualifications for accreditation should consult the more detailed publication A *Guide to Accreditation*. The criteria are being reviewed during 1993–4.

FUNDAMENTAL CRITERIA

To be accredited as a National Vocational Qualification, a qualification must be:

- based firmly on national standards required for performance in employment, and take proper account of future needs with particular regard to technology, markets and employment patterns;
- based on assessment of the outcomes of learning, specified independently of any particular mode, duration or location of learning;
- awarded on the basis of valid and reliable assessments made in such a way as to ensure that performance to the national standard can be achieved at work;
- free from barriers which restrict access and progression, and available to all those who are able to reach the required standard by whatever means;

* Reproduced by kind permission of the NCVQ

■ free from overt or covert discriminatory practices with regard to gender, age, race or creed and designed to pay due regard to the special needs of individuals.

I STATEMENTS OF COMPETENCE

1.1 All NVQs must consist of an agreed **statement of competence**, which should be determined or endorsed by a **Lead Body** with responsibility for defining, maintaining and improving national standards of performance in the sectors of employment where the competence is practised.

1.2 Responsibility for defining standards of competence rests with the recognised Lead Body, which should involve the appropriate employer, employee, professional, educational and training interests across the United Kingdom.

1.3 Competence must be specified in an NVQ statement of competence in a way which provides for **breadth** of application, so that:
   1.3.1 the area of competence covered has meaning and relevance in the sector or employment concerned;
   1.3.2 the competence covered is broadly comparable with other NVQs at the same level, particularly those in similar or adjacent areas;
   1.3.3 the range of competence is broad enough to give flexibility in employment and enhance employment opportunities;
   1.3.4 a basis for progression in both the sector concerned and related sectors is provided;
   1.3.5 adaptation to meet new and emerging occupational patterns is facilitated;
   1.3.6 there is no overt or covert discrimination against any section of the community in the wording or content of the statement of competence;
   1.3.7 the statement of competence is informed by relevant European developments on the comparability of qualifications.

1.4 The NVQ statement of competence should be derived from an analysis of functions within the area of competence to which it relates. It should reflect:
   1.4.1 competence relating to task management, safety and the

161

ability to deal with organisational environments, relationships with other people and unexpected events;

1.4.2   the ability to transfer the competence from place to place
and context to context;

1.4.3   the ability to respond positively to foreseeable changes in
technology, working methods, markets and employment
patterns and practices;

1.4.4   the underpinning skill, knowledge and understanding
which is required for effective performance in employment.

1.5 Where areas of competence are common to a number of employment sectors, Lead Bodies will be expected to use **generic** units of
competence whenever possible. These will often be produced by
appropriate cross-sectoral Lead Bodies.

1.6 Lead Bodies should also consider making explicit their requirements for transferable core **skills** in areas such as communication,
problem-solving and personal skills. The identification of such
requirements in NVQs may become essential at a later date.

2 FORMAT OF NVQ STATEMENT OF COMPETENCE

The NVQ statement of competence, which is the authoritative statement of the national standard of performance, must have the following components:

2.1 NVQ title, agreed by NVQ, which denotes the area of competence encompassed by the qualification, and locates it in the
NVQ framework;

2.2 **units of competence** are the main sub-divisions of an NVQ and
consist of a coherent group of elements of competence which has
meaning and independent value in the area of employment to
which the NVQ statement of competence relates. An NVQ
statement of competence will always have more than one unit.

2.2.1   units must be designed so that they can be offered for
separate assessment and certification, enabling them to be
recorded as credits in the national credit accumulation
and transfer system;

2.2.2   units should have titles which indicate the sub-areas of competence they cover.

2.3 **Elements of competence** are the sub-divisions of units and reflect those things a person should be able to do at work. They should:

  2.3.1   relate to what actually happens in work and not, for example, activities or skills which are only demonstrated on training programmes;

  2.3.2   be capable of demonstration and assessment;

  2.3.3   describe the result of what is done, not the procedures which may be used;

  2.3.4   not contain evaluative statements – these belong in performance criteria (see below);

  2.3.5   be expressed in language which makes sense to the people who will use them and which is unambiguous;

  2.3.6   be expressed in terms which permit application across different tasks, jobs, machines or organisational systems.

2.4 **Performance criteria** must accompany each element of competence and must contain evaluative statements which define the acceptable level of performance required in employment, normally in terms of its outcome, although some aspects of the way an activity is performed may also be critical. Performance criteria should:

  2.4.1   identify only the essential aspects of performance necessary for competence;

  2.4.2   be expressed so that assessments of candidates' performance can be made against them;

  2.4.3   form an unambiguous basis for the design of assessment systems and materials.

2.5 A **range statement** must also accompany each element. This should express the range of circumstances in which the competence must be applied, and may detail, for example, differences in physical location, employment contexts or machinery used.

2.6 **Assessment guidance**, although not part of the statement of competence, should also be provided by Lead Bodies for each element. In particular:

  2.6.1   where candidates may not be able to present sufficient evidence of competence through performance alone, it will often be necessary to collect evidence of their possession of the essential underpinning knowledge and understanding. Lead Bodies should help awarding bodies and providers to interpret their requirements by indicating what knowledge and understanding is considered essential;

2.6.2 where it may be impossible or uneconomic to assess performance across the whole of the range specified, the Lead Body should indicate the minimum requirements for performance evidence.

3 THE NVQ FRAMEWORK

3.1 The NVQ framework is the national system for ordering NVQs according to progressive levels of attainment and areas of competence. It provides a structure for accredited qualifications which indicates the relationship between them and helps identify progression routes.

3.2 The NVQ framework currently has five levels – the following definitions are intended to be indicative rather than prescriptive:

Level I: competence in the performance of a range of varied work activities, most of which are routine and predictable *or* which provide a broad foundation as a basis for progression.

Level II: competence in a significant range of varied work activities, performed in a variety of contexts. Some of the activities are complex or non-routine, and there is some individual responsibility or autonomy. Collaboration with others, perhaps through membership of a work group or team, may often be a requirement.

Level III: competence in a broad range of varied work activities performed in a wide variety of contexts and most of which are complex and non-routine. There is considerable responsibility and autonomy, and control or guidance of others is often required.

Level IV: competence in a broad range of complex, technical or professional work activities performed in a wide variety of contexts and with a substantial degree of personal responsibility and autonomy. Responsibility for the work of others and the allocation of resources is often present.

Level V: competence which involves the application of a significant range of fundamental principles and complex techniques
across a wide and often unpredictable variety of contexts.
Personal accountabilities for analysis and diagnosis, design, planning, execution and evaluation feature strongly, as do very
substantial personal autonomy and often significant responsibility
for the work of others and for the allocation of substantial
resources.

3.3 The design of qualifications should take account of the following
criteria:

   3.3.1   direct comparability of standards and levels will be
required between similar or adjacent occupational areas.
Comparison across a wider range of occupations will be
less exact, but the titles and levels of awards should
express general levels of attainment which are universally
understood;

   3.3.2   not all occupational areas will require all five levels – the
NCVQ will decide the level of an award based on the
advice of lead and awarding bodies, the above definitions
and the position of awards in similar areas of competence;

   3.3.3   NVQs should be constructed so that candidates can
progress from one level to the next and to related or adjacent areas of competence. It is not a requirement that all
candidates progress through all levels – many will acquire
the competences needed for NVQs at higher levels
through learning programmes which lead directly to them;

   3.3.4   NVQs may be made up of core units, which are common
to a number of NVQs, and units which are specific to a
single NVQ.

3.4 The NVQ framework provides a basis for making comparisons
with qualifications from other European member states. This will
enable NVQs to feature in future EEC comparability information
and provide the basis for future dialogue on converging European
standards.

3.5 The NVQ has developed a classification of areas of competence
which will form the horizontal axis of the national framework;
qualification titles and structures will increasingly be required to
conform to this.

4 ASSESSMENT
(SEE ALSO THE COMMON ACCORD, p 171)

4.1 Assessment for NVQs must be based on the statement of competence and the related assessment guidance. It is the process of collecting evidence and making judgements on whether or not performance criteria have been met. Before an NVQ can be awarded, candidates must have provided evidence that they have met the performance criteria for each element of competence specified.

4.2 Access to assessment for an NVQ should be available to all who have the potential to reach the standard required and be free from any barriers which restrict access. For example, assessment must be independent of:

■ the mode or location of learning;

■ upper and lower age limit, except where legal restraints make this necessary;

■ a specified period of time to be spent in education, training or work.

4.3 The NCVQ requires that:

4.3.1 the method of assessment used in any circumstances is valid and reliable;

4.3.2 alternative forms of assessment are provided where this will help to increase access to the qualification;

4.3.3 performance evidence should feature in the assessments for all elements of an NVQ;

4.3.4 performance must be demonstrated and assessed under conditions as close as possible to those under which it would normally be practised – preferably in the workplace;

4.3.5 if assessment in the workplace is not practicable, simulations, tests, projects or assignments may provide suitable evidence – but care must be taken to ensure that all elements and performance criteria have been covered, and that it is possible to predict that the competence assessed can be sustained in employment;

4.3.6 where performance evidence alone is limited and does not permit reliable inference of the possession of necessary knowledge and understanding, this must be separately assessed;

4.3.7   the method of assessment should always enable eligible candidates to demonstrate competence, and place no unnecessary additional demands on them;

4.3.8   some of the assessment for an NVQ may be conducted in a language other than English, provided that clear evidence is available that the candidate is competent in English to the standard required for competent performance throughout the UK;

4.3.9   provision should be made for the assessment of candidates with special needs, such as physical or sensory disabilities, who may need special help to undertake assessment. Where disabilities prevent candidates acquiring all the competences needed for the full NVQ, provision should be made for unit certification as appropriate;

4.3.10 a reliable system should be in place for recording evidence across the full range of circumstances in which the competence must be applied, as specified in the range statement.

5 AWARDING BODIES

5.1   The NCVQ approves bodies to award specific NVQs – it does not award them itself.

5.2   The NCVQ has the following general policies towards awarding bodies, in pursuit of its aims of rationalising and simplifying the system of vocational qualifications:

5.2.1   all NVQs in a given area of competence and at the same level must consist of a single national employment-led statement of competence provided by the appropriate Lead Body;

5.2.2   the NCVQ will encourage awarding bodies to develop their provision so that unnecessary duplication and overlap is avoided;

5.2.3   all bodies approved to award NVQs must participate in the NCVQ's system of credit accumulation and transfer.

5.3   An NVQ may be awarded by a single body, or a consortium of relevant bodies acting together: where a consortium is involved, the NCVQ will require a clear statement of the contributions to be made to the process of awarding the NVQ by each of the bodies concerned prior to accreditation. Single bodies or consortia must:

5.3.1   have recognised standing with appropriate employers and representatives of employees (including trades unions) in respect of the awards proposed for accreditation as shown by their acceptability within the relevant occupational group, sector of industry, commerce or public service, or profession;

5.3.2   provide assessment throughout England and Wales. Separate arrangements may be made for Northern Ireland;

5.3.3   undertake to contribute to the maintenance of the quality and relevance of the statements of competence which form part of the qualifications for which they seek accreditation;

5.3.4   agree to work with NCVQ and the Lead Bodies responsible for setting employment-led standards in the development and implementation of the NVQ framework;

5.3.5   be responsible for, and demonstrate capability in, the range of assessment required;

5.3.6   be responsible for the certification and administration of NVQs, including arrangements for credit accumulation and transfer;

5.3.7   have an equal opportunities policy and a means of monitoring its implementation; the policy and arrangements must be clearly communicated to candidates and to organisations involved in the delivery of training and education leading to the awards;

5.3.8   apply appropriate quality-assurance mechanisms;

5.3.9   agree to meet the conditions, regulations and guide-lines specified or issued by the NCVQ from time to time for accredited qualifications and awarding bodies, and pay the appropriate fees promptly to the NCVQ.

6 QUALITY ASSURANCE
(SEE ALSO THE COMMON ACCORD, p 171)

The NCVQ has an overriding responsibility for ensuring that awarding bodies have adequate arrangements and resources for quality assurance and that systems approved at the time of accreditation operate effectively and maintain the required performance throughout the period of accreditation. It will therefore require awarding bodies to have satisfactory arrangements for:

6.1 ensuring the competence of assessors;

6.2 monitoring or verifying that assessment is operated in accordance with their requirements, and consistently maintained at all assessment locations;

6.3 selecting, training and reviewing the performance of moderators/ verifiers;

6.4 instituting monitoring arrangements providing evidence of the effectiveness of their quality-assurance systems;

6.5 commissioning outside agencies to undertake evaluation where appropriate;

6.6 permitting NCVQ staff to attend meetings and/or training sessions for moderators/verifiers and assessors, and to see assessments taking place;

6.7 approving centres within which assessment will take place and ensuring they are capable of meeting all the requirements of the NVQ with regard to access, assessment and quality assurance;

6.8 administering, implementing, supporting and coordinating the above arrangements.

7 ACCREDITATION

7.1 Accreditation is the procedure by which the NCVQ:
- approves an **NVQ statement of competence** agreed by an appropriate Lead Body in an area of competence and at a level in the NVQ framework;
- approves an **awarding body** to offer, administer and maintain the quality of NVQs;
- approves awarding arrangements for specific NVQs, which may involve consortia of awarding bodies.

7.2 Awarding bodies must demonstrate to the satisfaction of the NCVQ that the qualification they submit meets the criteria in parts 1–7 of this section, and must accept contractually standard conditions which oblige them to:
7.2.1 include on each certificate awarded the designation 'National Vocational Qualification', the agreed title, the area of competence covered, the level in the NVQ frame-

work, the names of all bodies associated with the award, the date of the award, and the NCVQ insignia;

7.2.2 ensure that each candidate completing the requirements for an NVQ is awarded a certificate in the agreed form. No other certificate should be issued in respect of the NVQ;

7.2.3 issue separate certificates (records of achievement) for units in the agreed form for the purpose of credit accumulation;

7.2.4 observe such regulations, guidelines and criteria as may be issued by the NCVQ in relation to the accredited award;

7.2.5 take all necessary steps to maintain the quality of the qualification by monitoring the assessment of candidates and other appropriate means;

7.2.6 maintain, in collaboration with other relevant bodies, the award's relevance to employment needs, and not make any material change in its specification without the NCVQ's approval;

7.2.7 pay such fee to the NCVQ per certificate awarded as may be agreed in respect of each NVQ.

7.3 In addition, the NCVQ may require awarding bodies to meet **specific conditions** by agreeing a plan to introduce changes in an NVQ over a defined period.

7.4 Accreditation may be given for a maximum period of five years; but where specific conditions are attached, the period may be shorter.

7.5 Awarding bodies may apply for **re-accreditation** shortly before the expiry of the period of accreditation; in addition to examining applications against all the criteria in parts 1–5, the NCVQ will also consider awarding bodies' general performance in quality assurance, contract compliance and fee payment.

⋙ INFORMATION SECTION ⋘

The Common Accord

During 1992, officers of the National Council for Vocational Qualifications (NCVQ) worked with the main UK awarding bodies to develop the content of the Common Accord.

The Common Accord principles are intended to enhance the quality and cost effectiveness of NVQ assessment and verification processes operated by awarding bodies.

The Accord also aims to emphasise the coherence of the NVQ framework making it easier for users to understand NVQs.

The main features of the Accord are:

common terminology to describe the roles of the individuals and organisations in the assessment and quality assurance system

certification to national standards for assessors and verifiers

defined roles in quality assurance for both awarding bodies and the organisations which they approve to offer NVQs

explicit criteria for approving organisations to offer NVQs

quality assurance and control systems to ensure rigour and monitor equal opportunities implementation.

The Common Accord document was circulated for consultation at the end of 1992 and the published document reports that this 'generated support in terms of both its concept and content with the overwhelming majority of respondents agreeing the basic principles. Almost all respondents were in favour of the increased quality expected as a result of the accord' (NCVQ, 1993).

Perhaps one of the most interesting aspects of the document is the recognition by national bodies of 'the importance of reinforcing the concept of flexibility within the main principles of the Accord.' The document refers to the need for awarding bodies to have a 'sensible degree' of discretion to adapt elements of the Accord to circumstances.

To be more explicit, the document goes on to state that this may refer particularly to the frequency and duration of external verification visits and the length of time for which an external verifier is appointed.

There are many, perhaps, who would say that this degree of flexibility is inadequate. A number of difficulties experienced in implementation of NVQs go beyond those created by the frequency and duration of external verifier visits; they include difficulties with operating the **structure** of the NVQ, and with **interpretation** of the standards. Even more so, difficulties in **operationalising assessment practice,** particularly within a small company setting, are on the increase as the NVQ implementation rolls out.

Further difficulties appear to be created by the direct link to National Education and Training Targets (NETTs). The Training and Enterprise Councils (TECs) are supporting the NVQ implementation (with financial as well as practical support), but they too have targets to meet. These targets are quantitative – numbers of people achieving certification within a given timescale. Such quantitative targets do little to aid the **overall quality** which the Common Accord goes some way to help achieve.

However, it must also be recognised that the Common Accord is a step in the right direction to help deal with complaints of confusion and bureaucracy within the NVQ framework. Unless a common operational structure with common quality requirements and common terminology is established, it is unlikely that the NVQ system will be taken up by industry to the extent required by the National Targets.

DETAILS OF THE COMMON ACCORD

In outline, the Common Accord aims to provide:

Common Terminology:

The standard terms for the main functions and roles in the assessment and verification system are presented in the Common Accord as follows:

assessment is carried out by an **assessor**

internal verification is carried out by an **internal verifier**

external verification is carried out by an **external verifier**

approved centre – is approved by an awarding body to offer NVQ assessment. Each approved centre must have, or have access to, an appropriately qualified internal verifier.

In the case of a small centre (such as a small business), it is acceptable for the external verifier to carry out the functions of internal verification. It is not acceptable, however, to combine the functions of assessment and verification for the same assessment decision.

An approved centre is not necessarily a single site. Any company, for example, can become an approved centre; it is the organisation which is approved. A central site could operate a number of 'satellite' centres – which may be regional offices or operational units.

Conditional approval is not to be used as a mechanism within the quality assurance system. A centre must demonstrate how initial development leads to their meeting full approval criteria.

CERTIFICATION TO NATIONAL STANDARDS FOR ASSESSORS AND VERIFIERS

Following the launch of national standards for assessor and verifiers, which were developed by the Training and Development Lead Body (TDLB), the use of these standards was incorporated into quality assurance requirements for operational NVQ approved centres.

It is now a requirement that assessors and verifiers should establish their competence by holding certificates of unit credit in relevant national units. These targets for unit certification have been agreed, and published in the Common Accord, as follows:

Assessors   Unit D32 and/or D33
Internal verifiers   Unit **D34**, D32 and D33
External verifiers   Unit **D35**, D32 and D33.

The published requirement recognises that these targets are not immediately achievable and therefore states that **by 1995** (April), external and internal verifiers should be qualified with the single unit indicated in bold type above.

Also by April 1995, approval arrangements for centres should require that the centre has an action plan to certificate all existing and new assessors within an agreed timescale. From April 1995 onwards, all assessment decisions by assessors who are still working towards certification should normally be supported by an assessor or verifier who has gained certification.

The assessor and verifier units are available from all major awarding bodies. Each awarding body will have a full list of centres who are approved to provide development and assessment for assessors.

OCCUPATIONAL BACKGROUND OF ASSESSORS AND INTERNAL VERIFIERS

There has been much debate about the need for assessors and internal verifiers to be 'competent' in the occupational area for which they assess. NCVQ Guidance, published in the Common Accord, is as follows:

> Assessors, internal and external verifiers will all need some background which will enable them to judge whether a candidate's performance is meeting the specified standards of occupational competence. It is evident from the diversity of views expressed through consultation that the precise background that would be appropriate will vary between sectors and roles. A standard requirement for occupational background would thus be inappropriate. Instead, for each award, the awarding body should specify the occupational competence or experience considered necessary to perform each role.   (Common Accord, NCVQ, 1993, p 5)

Note that the phrase 'competence or experience' is used. A requirement for 'competence' would infer that any assessor would need to hold the relevant NVQ in order to assess in any particular occupational area.

DEFINED ROLES IN QUALITY ASSURANCE

The Common Accord defines these roles as follows:

Approved Centres
An approved centre takes charge of delivering assessment for (one or more designated) NVQs on a day-to-day basis. The centre should have effective internal procedures to ensure the quality and consistency of assessment. Centres are responsible for providing sufficient competent assessors and internal verifiers.

In the case of small centres, the individual who performs the internal verification function may come from another organisation – thus allowing for consortia arrangements.

Awarding Bodies
Awarding Bodies are responsible for verifying that assessment in an approved centre is carried out systematically, validly and to national standards. External verifiers are appointed by, and employees of,

awarding bodies. The awarding body will also to have an appeals procedure to deal with instances where a centre wishes to dispute approval decisions.

External Verifiers
External verifiers check the internal systems of the approved centres and also sample assessment practices and decisions. An external verifier also provides support and advice to centres and has the authority to recommend withdrawal of approval when circumstances merit this.

Explicit criteria for approving centres
Common criteria for approval of centres, agreed by all awarding bodies and published in the Common Accord relate to the following areas:

■ management systems
■ physical resources
■ staff resources
■ assessment
■ quality assurance and control
■ equal oportunities.

Each awarding body provides full details on their application for approval and the initial visit by the external verifier will help centres plan to meet all the specified criteria. All centres must be able to provide evidence, through action planning, that criteria can, indeed, be met. In the absence of such evidence approval will not be granted.

Full NVQs vs Units

The Common Accord contains recognition of the situation, in which some centres will not feel able to offer a full NVQ but should not be excluded from the approval process. It is a requirement of the Common Accord, therefore, that procedures are in place to allow centres to be approved to offer NVQ units.

Adding further NVQs to approved centre operations

A centre which is already approved to offer a particular NVQ may wish to add further NVQs (or units). In this instance, guidance is as follows:

a) where the occupational area, individuals involved as internal verifiers, and quality assurance systems are the same, then a simple application in writing may be appropriate.

b) where the quality assurance systems are the same as for an existing approval, but the NVQ is in a different area, then the awarding body may use abbreviated approval processes, carrying forward the appraisal made previously against certain approved criteria.

Duration of approval

Centre approval should be for a fixed period, taking account of the period of NCVQ accreditation for the award. External verifiers should also be appointed to centres for a fixed period.

Centre approval and verification criteria

A full set of criteria can be found in the Common Accord; the following provides a summary.

1. Management systems
   The centre must specify and maintain an effective system for managing NVQs.
2. Administrative arrangements
   Accurate records of the assessment of candidates must be maintained and awarding body administrative requirements fulfilled.
3. Physical resources
   Sufficient resources must be available to assess candidates for NVQs.
4. Staff resources
   Staff resources must be sufficient to deliver assessment for NVQs.
5. Assessment
   A system for valid and reliable assessment to national standards must be specified and maintained.
6. Quality assurance and control
   An effective system for quality assurance and control must be maintained.
7. Equal opportunities and access
   There must be a clear commitment to equal opportunities.

(Common Accord, NCVQ, 1993)

COSTS OF OPERATING NVQS

Costs for operating particular NVQs vary quite widely. The Common Accord gives no guidelines in this respect. However, in an attempt to provide some guidance, the following checklist will help you to ensure that you have considered all relevant aspects of implementation, including operating as an NVQ centre.

Centre approval costs:

Initial registration/approval fees
Most awarding bodies will charge an approval fee. This will cover the cost of visits by the external verifier during the first year, and may also cover the cost of issue of relevant materials (although this is an additional cost in some cases). Registration fees may vary from £150 to £1500 and are usually payable annually to relevant awarding bodies.

Candidate registration fees
There is usually a requirement to register individual candidates. This includes the cost of administration for entering the candidate details on the awarding body database and issue of registration documents (these can be a single form, or a log book). Costs again vary from around £15 to £50 per candidate. Check if this cost includes certification and the NCVQ levy.

Candidate log books/assessment packs
Issue of candidate materials may be included in the candidate registration fee (see above), but you need to ensure that you clarify this. For some awards, issue of awarding body log books and/or assessment packs is optional, for others it is mandatory. Candidate packs for the assessor awards are issued by (for example) City and Guilds at £5 each. The Institute of Training and Development provides a 'process pack' for candidates for the Training and Development awards at £36 each. The MCI Crediting Competence package costs £115 (average – this varies with the number of packs bought).

Costs of Assessment
You will need to consider the costs of assessment carefully. If you become an approved centre, your in-house assessors will need training and development; they too will need to be assessed against the national standards for assessors. Introducing competence-based assessment as an integral part of performance management takes time, and those undertaking the assessment and verification roles will need time to familiarise themselves with the new system and incorporate it into their everyday activity. The assessment process should,

eventually, become a full part of performance management, but should not add huge additional workloads.

If you do not become an NVQ Centre then you will need to consider how, where and what form of external assessment support you need to buy in. Check with the awarding bodies for approved centres and get quotes from several before deciding.

Financial support for the assessment process is available from TECs through the Skill Choice initiative – see p 99. Contact your local TEC for more information (see list of TECs in Appendix).

Certification costs

Both unit and full NVQ certification are available. Unit certification costs are usually between £2 and £9 per unit. A full NVQ certificate can cost between £20–£150. Awarding bodies calculate costs of verification and certification on the basis of the number of people who are likely to pass through the assessment and certification process in a given year. As commercial organisations, they too have to recover their costs. (It is important therefore that the development stage of NVQs bears this in mind and keeps administration to a minimum.)

GNVQs

Guidance in respect of GNVQs, which are currently only offered by BTEC, City and Guilds, and RSA is published separately and available from NCVQ.

Details of Industry Training Organisations and Lead Bodies

Sector	Industry Training Organisation/Lead Body	Coverage
Accounting	Lead Body for Accounting (Levels 2–4) Association of Accounting Technicians 154 Clerkenwell Road London EC1R 5AD (T) 071 837 8600	Accounting technicians Levels 2–4
Administration	Administration Lead Body The Institute of Chartered Secretaries and Administrators 16 Park Crescent London W1N 4AM (T) 071 580 4741 (F) 071 323 1132	Administration/Secretarial/ Information Processing
Agricultural & garden machinery	LB/ITO British Agricultural and Garden Machinery Association Church Street Rickmansworth Herts WD3 1RQ (T) 0923 720341 (F) 0923 896063	Agricultural and garden machinery supply and maintenance

Sector	Industry Training Organisation/Lead Body	Coverage
Agricultural co-operatives training council	ITO Training and Development Executive 23 Hanborough Business Park Long Hanborough Oxford OX8 8LH (T) 0993 883577 (F) 0993 883576	
Agricultural supply	ITO UK Agricultural Supply Trade Association 3 Whitehall Court London SW1A 2EQ (T) 071 930 3611 (F) 071 930 3952	
Agriculture	LB/ITO Agricultural Training Board Stoneleigh Park Pavilion National Agricultural Centre Stoneleigh Kenilworth Warwickshire CV8 2VG (T) 0203 696996 (F) 0203 696732	Agricultural and commercial horticultural services
Air transport	LB/ITO Aviation Training Association 125 London Road High Wycombe Bucks HP11 1BT (T) 0494 445262 (F) 0494 439984	Air transport services including group support
Air transport	LB/ITO Foreign Airlines Training Council c/o Air France 69 Boston Manor Road Brentford Middlesex TW8 9JQ (T) 081 750 4220	

Sector	Industry Training Organisation/Lead Body	Coverage
Animal care	Secretariat for Animal Care Lead Body Wood Green Animal Care Shelters Kings Bush Farm London Road Huntingdon Cambs PE18 8LJ (T) 0480 831177	Pet shops, catteries, kennels, groomers and zoos, vets
Arts and entertainments	LB/ITO Arts and Entertainment Training Council 3 St Peters Building York Street Leeds LS9 6AJ (T) 0532 448845	Performers (drama and dance), music, visual arts, creative writing
Atomic energy	ITO AEA Technology B149 Harwell Laboratories Oxon OX11 3HF (T) 0235 821111 (F) 0235 433788	
Bakers	LB Federation of Bakers 20 Bedford Square London WC1B 3HF (T) 071 637 7575	Large process baking bread/flour, confectionery production and distribution
Bakers	ITO National Association of Master Bakers 21 Baldock Street Ware Herts SG12 9DH (T) 0920 468061 (F) 0920 461632	

Sector	Industry Training Organisation/Lead Body	Coverage
Bakers	ITO Scottish Association of Master Bakers Atholl House 4 Torpichen Street Edinburgh EH3 8JQ (T) 031 229 1401 (F) 031 229 8239	
Banking	ITO Banking Industry Training Council 10 Lombard Street London EC2V 9AT (T) 071 626 9386 (F) 071 283 7037	Retail banking
Biscuit, cake, chocolate and confectionery	LB/ITO Biscuit, Cake, Chocolate and Confectionery Alliance 11 Green Street London W1Y 3RF (T) 071 629 8971 (F) 071 493 4885	
Books	LB/ITO Book House Training Centre 45 East Hill Wandsworth London SW18 2QZ (T) 081 874 2718 (F) 081 874 4790	
Booksellers	ITO Booksellers Association of Great Britain and Ireland Minster House 272 Vauxhall Bridge Road London SW1V 1BA (T) 071 834 5477 (F) 071 834 8812	

Sector	Industry Training Organisation/Lead Body	Coverage
Broadcasting and film	Broadcasting and Film Industry Lead Body Channel 4 TV 124 Horseferry Road London SW1P 2TX (T) 071 396 4444	All aspects of broadcasting including film, TV, radio and video
Broadcasting and film	ITO Skillset – Channel 4 TV 124 Horseferry Road London SW1P 2TX (T) 071 396 4444	Broadcast, film and video production
Brush	ITO British Brush Manufacturers Association Brooke House 4 The Lakes Bedford Road Northampton NN4 0YD (T) 0604 22023 (F) 0604 31252	Brush manufacture
Builders merchants	ITO Builders Merchants Federation Parnall House 5 Parnall Road Staple Tye Harlow Essex CM18 7PP (T) 0279 439654 (F) 0279 430127	Wholesale distribution of building materials
Building management	LB Institute of Maintenance and Building Management Keets House 30 East Street Farnham Surrey GU9 7SW (T) 0252 710994	Maintenance and servicing of buildings, estates, industrial and commercial properties

Sector	Industry Training Organisation/Lead Body	Coverage
Building products	LB/ITO Building Products Training Council c/o CITB Radnor House 1272 London Road London SW16 4EL (T) 081 679 8511 (F) 081 764 6241	Brick manufacture
Building societies	LB British Building Societies Association 3 Savile Row London W1X 1AF (T) 071 437 0655	Building Societies
Bus and coach	LB Bus and Coach Training Ltd Gable House 40 High Street Rickmansworth Herts WD3 1ER (T) 0923 896607 (F) 0923 896881	Bus and coach operations
Caravan	Caravan Industry Training Organisation 88 Victoria Road Aldershot Hants GU11 1SS (T) 0252 344170	Manufacture and selling of caravans/operation of caravan parks
Care	LB Care Sector Consortium (NHSTD) St Bartholomews Court 18 Christmas Street Bristol BS1 5BT (T) 0272 291029	Public and private sectors of health and social services and voluntary sector

Sector	Industry Training Organisation/Lead Body	Coverage
Carpet	Carpet Industry Training Council c/o BAGMA 4th Floor Royalty House 72 Dean Street London W1V 5HB (T) 071 734 9853 (F) 071 734 9856	Carpet manufacture
Cement	LB/ITO British Cement Association Wexham Springs Slough SL3 6PL (T) 0753 662727 (F) 0753 660399/660499	Cement manufacture and distribution
Ceramic	LB/ITO Association of Ceramic Training and Development 2nd Floor Federation House Station Road Stoke-on-Trent ST4 2SA (T) 0782 745335 (F) 0782 745336	Ceramic goods manufacture
Chemical	LB/ITO Chemical Industries Association Ltd Kings Building Smith Square London SW1P 3JJ (T) 071 834 3399 (F) 071 834 4469	
Civil engineering	LB CISC The Building Centre 26 Store Street London WC1E 7BT (T) 071 323 5270	The Industry standing conference for Architecture, Building and Quantity Surveying, Building and Civil Engineering

Sector	Industry Training Organisation/Lead Body	Coverage
Civil service	Cabinet Office (OMCS) Development Division Horse Guards Road London SW1P 3AL (T) 071 273 6519 (F) 071 270 6301	
Cleaning	ITO Cleaning and Support Services Association Suite 73/74 The Hop Exchange 24 Southwark Street London SE1 1TY (T) 071 403 2747 (F) 071 403 1984	Cleaning
Cleaning	Cleaning Lead Body Hill House Skinners Lane Wroxham Norwich N12 8SJ (T) 0603 784547	Cleaning
Clothing	LB/ITO CAPITB Trust 80 Richardshaw Lane Pudsey Leeds LS28 6BN (T) 0532 393355 (F) 0532 393155	Clothing and related products manufacture
Coal	ITO British Coal Eastwood Hall Mansfield Road Eastwood Nottingham NG16 3EB (T) 0773 532111 (F) 0773 532111	Extraction of coal

Sector	Industry Training Organisation/Lead Body	Coverage
Concrete	Precast Concrete Industry Training Association 7th Floor 60 Charles Street Leicester LE1 1FB (T) 0533 512442 (F) 0533 512683	
Concrete	Autoclaved Aerated Concrete Products Association c/o Eaton Management Services Ltd Eaton House 96a New Walk Leicester LE1 1FB (T) 0533 471887	
Conservation	LB COSQUEC The Red House Pillows Green Staunton Glos GL19 3NU (T) 0452 840825 (F) 0452 849824	Land based industries and urban conservation
Construction	LB/ITO Construction Industry Training Board Bircham Newton Near Kings Lynn Norfolk PE31 6RH (T) 0553 776677 (F) 0553 692226	All aspects of construction
Cosmetics	ITO Cosmetics, Toiletry and Perfumery Association 35 Dover Street London W1X 3RA (T) 071 491 8891 (F) 071 493 8061	

Sector	Industry Training Organisation/Lead Body	Coverage
Craft	LB Craft Occupational Standards Board Enterprise House 25–29 Cherry Orchard Lane Salisbury SP2 7LD (T) 0722 339870	Craft industries
Drinks	LB/ITO British Soft Drinks Association 20–22 Stukeley Street London WC2B 5LR (T) 071 430 0356	Manufacture of soft drinks and mineral water
Electrical installation	Electrical Installation & Engineering ITO ESCA House 34 Palace Court London W2 4HY (T) 071 229 1266 (F) 071 221 7344	Electrical contracting
Electrical and electronics servicing	Electrical & Electronics Servicing LB Savoy Hill House Savoy Hill London WC2R 0BS (T) 071 836 3357 (F) 071 497 9007	Servicing of consumer electronic goods, domestic appliances and vending machines
Electricity	LB/ITO The Electricity Training Association 30 Millbank London SW1P 4RD (T) 071 834 2333 (F) 071 233 6640	Electricity generation, distribution and supply

Sector	Industry Training Organisation/Lead Body	Coverage
Electronic office systems	Electronic Office Systems Maintenance LB c/o EEB Savoy Hill House Savoy Hill London WC2R 0BS (T) 071 836 3357 (F) 071 233 6640	Office equipment maintenance/servicing
Energy efficiency	EESAG Energy Efficiency Office Department of Environment 1 Palace Street London SW1E 5HE	
Engineering construction	Engineering Contruction ITB Blue Court Kings Langley Hertfordshire WD4 8JP (T) 0923 260000 (F) 0923 270969	Not an LB or an ITO
Engineering	LB/ITO The Engineering Training Authority Vector House 41 Clarendon Road Watford Hertfordshire WD1 1HS (T) 0923 238441 (F) 0923 256086	Engineering Industry with emphasis on manufacture
Engineering	LB Engineering Occupation Standards Group 10 Maltravers Street London WC2R 3ER	

Sector	Industry Training Organisation/Lead Body	Coverage
Engineering	LB/ITO Marine and Engineering Training Association Rycote Place 30–38 Cambridge Street Aylesbury Bucks HP20 1RS (T) 0296 434943 (F) 0296 437124	Engineering with emphasis on shipbuilding and design
Engineering manufacture	LB Standard Conference for Engineering Manufacture c/o The Institution of Electrical Engineers Savoy Place London WC2R 0RL	
Engineering services	Standard Conference for Engineering Services c/o The Institution of Marine Engineers The Memorial Building 76 Mark Lane London EC3R 7JN	
Estate agents	LB Residential Estate Agents Training & Education Association (REATEA) The Avenue Brampford Speke Nr Exeter EX5 5DW (T) 0392 841194	
Extraction	LB Standing Conference for Extraction & Processing c/o The Institution of Chemical Engineers Davis Building 165–171 Railway Terrace Rugby CV21 3HQ	

Sector	Industry Training Organisation/Lead Body	Coverage
Extractive	LB/ITO China Clay & Ball Clay Industry Training Board John Keay House St Austell Cornwall PL25 4DJ (T) 0726 74482 (F) 0726 623 019	Extraction of china clay and ball clay
Extractive	Mining Industry Lead Body c/o Education and Training Branch Eastwood Coal Eastwood Hall Eastwood Nottingham NG16 3EB (T) 0773 532111	Mining activities
Extractive	LB/ITO Quarry Products Training Council Sterling House Station Road Gerrards Cross Bucks SL9 8HT (T) 0753 891808 (F) 0753 891132	Quarrying and related activities
Extractive	LB/ITO Silica and Moulding Sands Association 19 Warwick Street Rugby Warwickshire CV21 3DH (T) 0788 573041 (F) 0788 560316	Extraction of special sands

Sector	Industry Training Organisation/Lead Body	Coverage
Fabric care	ITO Fabric Care Research Association Forest House Laboratories Knaresborough Road Harrogate HG2 7LZ (T) 0423 885977 (F) 0423 880045 LB TRICE c/o Fabric Care Research Association	Dry cleaners, launderers, textile rental and launderettes
Fencing	ITO National Fencing Training Authority Board Suite 18 I-Mex Business Park Snobhall Road Burton on Trent Staffordshire DE14 2AU (T) 0283 512611 (F) 0283 515049	
Fibre cement	ITO Fibre Cement Manufacturers' Association PO Box 117 Hexham Northumberland NE46 3LQ (T) 0434 601393 (F) 0434 608874	
Fibreboard packaging	LB/ITO British Fibreboard Packaging Association (BFPA) 2 Saxon Court Freeschool Street Northampton NN1 1ST (T) 0604 21002 (F) 0604 20636	Fibreboard conversion and manufacture

Sector	Industry Training Organisation/Lead Body	Coverage
Financial services	Occupational Standards Council CREATE 2 Holly Hill Vauxhall Lane Southborough Tunbridge Wells Kent TN4 0XD	
Fire	Fire Industry Lead Body Secretariat The Loss Prevention Council 140 Aldersgate Street London EC1A 4HY (T) 071 606 1050 (F) 071 606 1050	Fire engineering and equipment
Fire	Emergency Fire Services Lead Body Home Office Room 935 Queen Anne's Gate London EC1A 9AT (T) 071 273 3925	Fire fighting and associated operations
Floristry	LB Floristry Industry Vocational Quals Group College of NE London Tottenham Centre High Road Tottenham London N15 4RU (T) 081 802 3111	Preparation and sale of flowers and foliage for display and decoration
Food	LB Training & Careers Executive Food Manufacturing Council for Industrial Training 6 Catherine Street London WC2B 5JJ (T) 071 836 2460 (F) 071 836 0580	Food manufacture

Sector	Industry Training Organisation/Lead Body	Coverage
Footwear	LB/ITO British Footwear Manufacturers' Federation Royalty House 72 Dean Street London W1V 5HB (T) 071 734 0951 (F) 071 494 1300	Footwear manufacture
Forensic science	LB Forensic Science Service Priory Hill Gooch Street North Birmingham B5 6QQ (T) 021 666 6606	All forensic science activities and associated activities
Forestry	LB/ITO Forestry & Arboriculture Safety Training Council Forestry Commission 231 Corstorphine Road Edinburgh EH12 7AT (T) 031 334 8083 (F) 031 334 3047	Forestry work, harvesting, arboriculture, silviculture
Frozen food	LB/ITO UK Association of Frozen Food Producers 1 Green Street London W1Y 3RG (T) 071 629 0655 (F) 071 499 9095	Production of frozen foods and ice cream
Furniture	LB/ITO British Furniture Manufacturers Fed. 30 Harcourt Street London W1H 2AA (T) 071 724 0854 (F) 071 706 1924	Furniture manufacture

DETAILS OF INDUSTRY LEAD BODIES

Sector	Industry Training Organisation/Lead Body	Coverage
Game keeping and fish husbandry	LB Valley Farm Stoke Andover ST11 0NR (T) 0264 738313	All aspects of fish husbandry & gamekeeping
Health service	ITO Management Education Division Scottish Health Service Common Services Agency Crewe Road South Edinburgh EH4 2FL (T) 031 332 2335 (F) 031 315 2369	Health Service employees in Scotland
Heating and ventilating	ITO Engineering Services Training 　Trust Ltd ESCA House 34 Palace Court Bayswater London W2 4JG (T) 071 229 2488 (F) 072 727 9266	Heating, ventilating and refrigeration services
Horse	LB/ITO Joint National Horse Education 　& Training Council The Northern Racing School The Stables Rossington Hall Great North Road Doncaster DN11 0HN (T) 0302 864242 (F) 0302 864151	Horse industry in GB including racing
Horticulture	Amenity Horticulture Lead Body Local Govt Management Board Arndale House Arndale Centre Luton LU1 2TS (T) 0582 451166	All aspects of non commercial horticulture

Sector	Industry Training Organisation/Lead Body	Coverage
Hotel & catering	LB/ITO The Hotel & Catering Training Company International House High Street Ealing London W5 5DB (T) 081 579 2400 (F) 081 840 6217	
Housing	LB Housing Sector Consortium Arndale House Arndale Centre Luton Beds LU1 2TS (T) 0582 451166	Management, maintenance and development of housing by Local Authorities, Housing Associations and other bodies
Information technology	Information Technology ITO 16 South Molton Street London W1Y 1DE (T) 071 355 4924 (F) 071 495 8613	Information Technology
Insulation	LB/ITO Insulation and Environmental Training Agency Unit 125, Cannock Chase Enterprise Centre Walkers Rise Hednesford Staffordshire WS12 5QU (T) 0534 871337 (F) 0534 871153	Thermal insulation
Insurance	LB/ITO Insurance Industry Training Council 271a High Street Orpington Kent BR6 0NW (T) 0689 896711 (F) 0689 896905	Insurance services

DETAILS OF INDUSTRY LEAD BODIES

Sector	Industry Training Organisation/Lead Body	Coverage
International trade	International Trade and Services Lead Body British Chambers of Commerce 4 Westwood House Westwood Business Park Coventry CV4 8HS (T) 0203 694492 (F) 0203 694690	
Jewellery	LB National Joint Working Group for the Jewellery and Allied Industries British Jewellers Association 10 Vyse Street Birmingham B18 6LT	
Knitting, lace and narrow fabric	ITO Knitting, Lace and Narrow Fabric Industries Training Resources Agency 7 Gregory Boulevard Nottingham NG7 6LD (T) 0602 605330 (F) 0605 625450	All aspects of knitting, lace and narrow fabric manufacture
Landscaping	British Landscaping ITO Henry Street Keighley West Yorkshire BD21 3DR (T) 0535 606139 (F) 0535 610269	
Languages	Languages Lead Body c/o CILT 20 Bedfordbury London WC2N 4LB (T) 071 379 5134 (F) 071 379 5082	

Sector	Industry Training Organisation/Lead Body	Coverage
Law	ITO Professional Standards & Development Directorate Law Society Isley Court Redditch Worcestershire B98 0TD (T) 071 242 1222	All staff employed in solicitors' offices in England and Wales
Leather	LB/ITO British Leather Confederation Leather Trade House Kings Park Road Moulton Park Northampton NN3 1JD (T) 0604 494131 (F) 0604 648220	Leather production
Leather goods	Leather Goods ITO Walsall Chamber of Commerce Wednesbury Training Centre St Pauls Road Wood Green Wednesbury West Midlands WS10 9QX (T) 021 556 0959 (F) 021 556 2049	Leather goods manufacture GB
Library	LB The Library Association 7 Ridgmount Street London WC1E 7AE (T) 071 636 7543	
Lift truck	LB Joint Industry Council for Lift Truck Operating Standards & VQs Scammell House High Street Ascot Berkshire SL5 7JK (T) 0344 23800	

DETAILS OF INDUSTRY LEAD BODIES

Sector	Industry Training Organisation/Lead Body	Coverage
Local authorities	ITO Convention of Scottish Local Authorities Rosebery House 9 Haymarket Terrace Edinburgh EH12 5XZ (T) 031 346 1222 (F) 031 346 0055	
Local government	Local Government Management Board 4th Floor Arndale House Arndale Centre Luton LU1 2TS (T) 0582 451166 (F) 0582 412525	
Man-made fibres	Man Made Fibres ITO Central House Gate Lane Sutton Coldfield West Midlands B73 5TS (T) 021 355 7022 (F) 021 355 7090	Man-made fibres manufacture
Marine	ITO British Marine Federation Meadlake Place Thorpe Lea Road Egham Surrey TW20 8HE (T) 0784 473377 (F) 0784 439678	Boat building and repair, outfitting, marine activities, boat hiring etc
Marketing	LB Marketing Services Board 49a High Street Yeadon Leeds West Yorkshire LS 19 7SP (T) 0532 508955	

Sector	Industry Training Organisation/Lead Body	Coverage
Meat	Meat Industry Training Organisation PO Box 661 Winterhill House Snowdon Drive Milton Keynes MK6 1BB (T) 0908 609829 (F) 0908 609221	Meat processing and whole-sale (England, Scotland and Wales) Meat retail (England and Wales)
Meat	ITO Scottish Federation of Meat Traders Association Perth Livestock Market 8 Needless Road Perth PH2 0JW (T) 0738 32984/37785 (F) 0738 441059	Meat retail (Scotland)
Mechanical Engineering	LB Mechanical Engineering Services Consortium Gear House Salt Meadows Road Gateshead NE8 3AH (T) 091 490 1155 (F) 091 477 5737	
Merchant Navy	LB/ITO Merchant Navy Training Board 2/5 Minories London EC3N 1BJ (T) 071 702 1100 (F) 071 626 8135	
Millers	LB/ITO Incorporated National Association of British and Irish Millers 21 Arlington Street London SW1A 1RN (T) 071 493 2521 (F) 071 493 6785	

Sector	Industry Training Organisation/Lead Body	Coverage
Motor	LB/ITO Motor Industry Training Standards Council 201 Great Portland Street London W1N 6AB (T) 071 436 6373 (F) 071 436 5108	
Museum	LB/ITO Museum Training Institute Kershaw House 55 Well Street Bradford BD1 5PS (T) 0274 391056 (F) 0274 394890	Museums, Galleries and Heritage
Newspaper	ITO The Newspaper Publishers' Association 34 Southwark Bridge Road London SE1 (T) 071 928 6928 (F) 071 401 2428/071 928 2067	
Newspaper	LB/ITO The Newspaper Society Bloomsbury House Bloomsbury Square 74–77 Great Russell Street London WC1B 3DA (T) 071 636 7014 (F) 071 631 5119	
Nuclear Fuels	LB/ITO British Nuclear Fuels Plc Risley Warrington WA3 6AS (T) 0925 832374 (F) 0925 822711	Manufacture and suppliers of nuclear fuels

Sector	Industry Training Organisation/Lead Body	Coverage
Packaging	ITO British Box and Packaging Association Papermakers House Rivenhall Road Swindon SN5 7BE (T) 0793 886086 (F) 0783 886182	Flat card packaging
Paintmakers	ITO Paintmakers Association of Great Britain 6th Floor Alembic House 93 Albert Embankment London SE1 7TY (T) 071 582 1185 (F) 071 735 0616	
Paper & Board	LB/ITO British Paper & Board Industry Federation Papermakers House Rivenhill Road Westlea Swindon SN5 7BE (T) 0793 886086 (F) 0793 886182	
Paper Merchants	ITO National Association of Paper Merchants Hamilton Court Gogmore Lane Chertsey Surrey KT16 9AF (T) 0932 5697978 (F) 0932 569749	

DETAILS OF INDUSTRY LEAD BODIES

Sector	Industry Training Organisation/Lead Body	Coverage
Pensions	LB The Pensions Management Institute PMI House 4–10 Artillery Lane London E1 7LS (T) 071 247 1452 (F) 071 375 0603	
Periodicals	LB/ITO Periodicals Training Council Imperial House 15–19 Kingsway London WC2B 6UN (T) 071 836 8798 (F) 071 379 5661	
Personnel	Personnel Lead Body Secretariat c/o Institute of Personnel Management IPM House Camp Road Wimbledon London SW19 4UX (T) 081 946 9100	
Pest Control	Pest Control Lead Body British Pest Control Association 3 St James' Court Friar Gate Derby DE1 1ZU (T) 0332 294288 (F) 0332 295904	
Petroleum	Offshore Petroleum ITO Forties Road Montrose Angus DD10 9ET (T) 0674 671666 (F) 0674 75306	

Sector	Industry Training Organisation/Lead Body	Coverage
Petroleum	LB/ITO Petroleum Employers' Skills Council Suite 1 Morley House 314 Regent Street London W1R 5AB (T) 071 255 2335 (F) 071 255 1828	
Pharmaceutical	LB/ITO Association of the British Pharmaceutical Industry 12 Whitehall London SW1A 2DY (T) 071 930 3477 (F) 071 930 3290	
Photography	LB/ITO Photography & Photographic Processing Peel Place 50 Carver Street Hockley Birmingham B1 3AS (T) 021 212 0299	
Plumbing	LB/ITO British Plumbing Employers Council c/o SNIPEF 2 Walker Street Edinburgh EH3 7LB (T) 031 225 2255 (F) 031 226 7638	
Polymer	LB/ITO British Polymer Training Association Coppice House Halesfield 7 Telford Shropshire TF7 4NA (T) 0952 587020 (F) 0952 582065	

Sector	Industry Training Organisation/Lead Body	Coverage
Ports	British Ports ITO PO Box 555 Bury St Edmunds Suffolk IP28 6QG (T) 0284 811555 (F) 0284 811554	
Post	ITO Post Office Management College Coton House Rugby CV23 0AA (T) 0788 574111 (F) 0788 579705	
Road Haulage	Road Haulage Industry Training and Standards Council Capitol House Empire Way Wembley Middlesex HA9 0NG (T) 081 900 2746 (F) 081 903 4113	
Saddlers	LB Worshipful Company of Saddlers 40 Gutter Lane London EC2V 6BR (T) 071 726 8661/6 (F) 071 600 0386	Saddle manufacture
Sales	Sales Lead Body Direct Selling Association 29 Floral Street London WC2E 9DP (T) 071 497 1234 (F) 071 497 3144	

Sector	Industry Training Organisation/Lead Body	Coverage
Sawmillers	ITO UK Softwood Sawmillers Association Silverbank Sawmills Banchory AB31 3PY (T) 03302 3366 (F) 03302 5018	
Screen Printing	LB Screen Printing Association (UK) Limited 7a West Street Reigate Surrey RH2 9BL (T) 0737 240792	
Sea Fish	LB/ITO Sea Fish Industry Authority Sea Fish House St Andrews' Dock Hull HU3 4QE (T) 0482 27837 (F) 0482 223310	
Security	Security ITO and Lead Body Security House Barbourne Road Worcester WR1 1RS (T) 0905 20004 (F) 0905 613625	
Security services	Security Services LB Secretariat IPSA 3 Dendy Road Paignton Devon TQ4 5DB (T) 0803 554849 (F) 0803 529203	

Sector	Industry Training Organisation/Lead Body	Coverage
Security and Emergency systems	ITO NACOSS Queensgate House 14 Cookham Road Maidenhead Berkshire SL6 8AJ (T) 0628 37512 (F) 0628 773367	
Ship	ITO Ship Safe Training Group c/o Crescent Shipping 11–13 Canal Road Rochester Kent ME2 4DS (T) 0634 290092 (F) 0634 716019	
Shoe repair	Shoe Repair ITO 76 The Parade Sutton Coldfield West Midlands B72 1PD (T) 021 355 2033	Shoe repair
Sign	LB British Sign Association Swan House 207 Balham High Road London SW17 7BQ (T) 081 675 7241	
Small firms	Small Firms Lead Body 140 Lower Marsh Westminster Bridge London SE1 7AE (T) 071 928 9272	

Sector	Industry Training Organisation/Lead Body	Coverage
Soap and detergent	LB/ITO Soap and Detergent Industry Association PO Box 9 Hayes Gate House Hayes Middlesex UB4 0JD (T) 081 573 7992 (F) 081 561 5077	
Sports surfaces	Synthetic Sports Surfaces Training Organisation PO Box 91 Leicester LE4 4EJ (T) 0533 677588 (F) 0533 677590	
Sports and recreation	Local Government Management Board Arndale House Arndale Centre Luton LU1 2TS (T) 0582 451166	
Steel	LB/ITO British Steel Plc Central Training Services Ashorne Hill Management College Leamington Spa Warwickshire CV33 9QW (T) 0962 651321	
Steel	ITO Steel Training Limited Staybrite Works Weedon Street Sheffield S9 2FU (T) 0742 446833/448088 (F) 0742 562855	

DETAILS OF INDUSTRY LEAD BODIES

Sector	Industry Training Organisation/Lead Body	Coverage
Sugar	LB/ITO United Kingdom Sugar Industry Association British Sugar PO Box 26 Oundle Street Peterborough PE2 9QV (T) 0733 63171 (F) 0733 317537	
Telecommunications	ITO Telecommunications Industry Association 20 Drakes Mews Crownhill Milton Keynes MK8 0ER (T) 0908 265090 (F) 0908 263852	
Telecommunications	LB Dacon House Presley Way Crownhill Milton Keynes MK8 0HD (T) 0908 265500	
Textiles	Cotton & Allied Textiles ITO Reedham House 31 King Street West Manchester ME 2PF (T) 061 832 9291 (F) 061 833 1740	
Textiles	LB National Textile Training Group c/o KLITRA 7 Gregory Boulevard Nottingham NG7 6LD (T) 0602 605330 (F) 0602 625450	Textile industry

Sector	Industry Training Organisation/Lead Body	Coverage
Theatre technicians	LB Arts and Entertainment Technical Training Initiative Silverton College High Street Broughton Hampshire SO20 8AD (T) 0794 301386	
Timber	ITO The British Timber Merchants Association Stocking Lane Hughenden Valley High Wycombe Buckinghamshire HP14 4JZ (T) 0494 563602 (F) 0494 565487	
Timber	LB/ITO Timber Trade Training Association Clareville House 26/27 Oxendon Street London SW1Y 4EL (T) 071 839 1891 (F) 071 930 0094	
Tabacco	Tobacco Industry Training Organisation Glen House Stag Place London SW1E 5AG (T) 071 828 2803 (F) 071 630 9638	Tabacco and snuff manufacture
Tool hire	LB Hire Association Europe Limited 722 College Road Erdington Birmingham B44 0AJ (T) 021 377 7707 (F) 021 382 1743	

Sector	Industry Training Organisation/Lead Body	Coverage
Training and development	TDLB Secretariat c/o NCITO 5 George Lane Royston Herts SG8 9AR (T) 0763 247285	
Travel agents	1 – Travel Services – LB 2 – Association of British Travel Agents – ITO National Training Board Waterloo House 11–17 Chertsey Road Woking Surrey GU21 5AL (T) 0483 727321 (F) 0483 756698	
Vets/vet nurses	Veterinary Lead Body The Royal College of Veterinary Surgeons 32 Belgrave Square London SW1X 8QP (T) 071 235 4971 (F) 071 245 6100	Vets, Veterinary Nurses and Farriers
Wallcovering	ITO Wallcovering Manuf Assoc of Great Britain Alembic House 93 Albert Embankment London SE1 7TY (T) 071 582 1185 (F) 071 735 0616	
Warehouse	Warehouse ITO Walter House 418–422 Strand London WC2R 0PT (T) 071 836 5522 (F) 071 379 6904	

Sector	Industry Training Organisation/Lead Body	Coverage
Waste	Waste Management Industry Training and Advisory Board 9 Saxon Court St Peters Gardens Northampton NN1 1SX (T) 0604 20426 (F) 0604 21339	
Water	ITO/LB Board of Education & Training for the Water Industry 1 Queen Anne's Gate London SW1H 9BT (T) 071 957 4567 (F) 071 233 0153	
Waterway	ITO British Waterways Greycaine Road Watford Herts WD2 1JR (T) 0923 226422 (F) 0923 226081	
Wholesale	LB National Wholesale Training Council I-Mex House 40 Princess Street Manchester M1 6DE (T) 061 237 9199 (F) 061 237 9399	
Wool	ITO Confederation of British Wool Textiles Ltd Merryvale House Roydsdale Way Bradford BD4 6SB (T) 0274 652207 (F) 0274 652218	Wool textiles

Sector	Industry Training Organisation/Lead Body	Coverage
Wool (Scotland)	ITO Scottish Woollen Industry c/o Scottish Textile Association 45 Moray Place Edinburgh EH3 6EQ (T) 031 225 9094 (F) 031 220 4942	Wool textiles (Scotland)

Training and Enterprise Councils

TEC Name	Address	Tel & Fax No
Avon TEC	PO Box 164 St Lawrence House 29–31 Broad Street Bristol BS99 7HR	(T) 0272 277116 (F) 0272 226664
AZTEC	Manorgate House 2 Manorgate Road Kingston upon Thames KT2 7AL	(T) 081 547 3934 (F) 081 547 3884
Barnsley/ Doncaster TEC	Conference Centre Eldon Street Barnsley S70 2JL	(T) 0226 248088 (F) 0226 291625
Bedfordshire TEC	Woburn Court 2 Railton Road Woburn Industrial Estate Kempstone Bedfordshire MK42 7PN	(T) 0234 843100 (F) 0234 843211
Birmingham TEC	Chaplin Court 80 Hurst Street Birmingham B5 4TG	(T) 021 622 4419 (F) 021 622 1600

TEC Name	Address	Tel & Fax No
Bolton Bury TEC	Clive House Clive Street Bolton BL1 1ET	(T) 0204 397350 (F) 0204 363212
Bradford & District TEC	Fountain Hall Fountain Street Bradford BD1 3RA	(T) 0274 723711 (F) 0274 370980
Calderdale/ Kirklees TEC	Park View House Woodvale Office Park Woodvale Road Brighouse HD6 4AB	(T) 0484 400770 (F) 0484 400672
CAMBSTEC	Units 2–3 Trust Court Chivers Way The Vision Park Histon Cambridge CB4 4PW	(T) 0223 235633/635 (F) 0223 235631/632.
Central England TEC	The Oaks Clewes Road Redditch B98 7ST	(T) 0527 545415 (F) 0527 543032
CENTEC	12 Grosvenor Crescent London SW1X 7EE	(T) 071 411 3500 (F) 071 411 3555
CEWTEC	Block 4 Woodside Business Park Birkenhead Wirral L41 1EH	(T) 051 650 0555 (F) 051 650 0777

TEC Name	Address	Tel & Fax No
CLINTEC	80 Great Eastern Street London EC2A 3DP	(T) 071 324 2424 (F) 071 324 2400
County Durham TEC	Valley Street North Darlington DL1 1TJ	(T) 0325 351166 (F) 0325 381362
Coventry & Warwickshire TEC	Brandon Court Progress Way Coventry CV3 2TE	(T) 0203 635666 (F) 0203 450242
Cumbria TEC	Venture House Regents Court Guard Street Workington Cumbria CA14 4EW	(T) 0900 66991 (F) 0900 604027
Devon & Cornwall TEC	Foliot House Brooklands Budshead Road Crown Hill Plymouth PL6 5XR	(T) 0752 767929 (F) 0752 770925
Dorset TEC	25 Oxford Road Bournemouth BH8 8EY	(T) 0202 299284 (F) 0202 299457
Dudley TEC	Dudley Court South Waterfront East Level Street Brierley Hill West Midlands DY5 1XN	(T) 0384 485000 (F) 0384 483399

TEC Name	Address	Tel & Fax No
ELTEC	Red Rose Court Petre Road Clayton Business Park Clayton-Le-Moor Lancashire BB5 5JR	(T) 0254 301333 (F) 0254 399090
Essex TEC	Redwing House Hedgerows Business Park Colchester Road Chelmsford Essex CM2 5PB	(T) 0245 450123 (F) 0245 451430
Gloucestershire TEC	Conway House 33–35 Worcester Street Gloucester GL1 3AJ	(T) 0452 524488 (F) 0452 307144
Greater Nottingham TEC	Marina Road Castle Marina Park Nottingham NG7 1TN	(T) 0602 413313 (F) 0602 484589
Greater Peterborough TEC	Unit 4 Blenheim Court Peppercorn Close off Lincoln Road Peterborough PE1 2DU	(T) 0733 890808 (F) 0733 890809
Gwent TEC	Glyndwr House Unit B2 Cleppa Park Newport Gwent NP9 1YE	(T) 0633 817777 (F) 0633 810980

TEC Name	Address	Tel & Fax No
Hampshire TEC	25 Thackeray Mall Fareham Hampshire PO 16 0PQ	(T) 0329 230099 (F) 0329 237733
HAWTEC	Haswell House St Nicholas Street Worcester WR1 1UW	(T) 0905 723200 (F) 0905 613338
Heart of England TEC	26/27 The Quadrant Abingdon Science Park off Barton Lane Abingdon OX14 3YS	(T) 0235 553249 (F) 0235 555706
Hertfordshire TEC	New Barnes Mill Cotton Mill Lane St Albans Herts AL1 2HA	(T) 0727 852313 (F) 0727 841449
Humberside TEC	The Maltings Silvester Square Silvester Street Hull HU1 3HL	(T) 0482 226491 (F) 0482 213206
Kent TEC	5th Floor Mountbatten House 28 Military Road Chatham Kent ME4 4JE	(T) 0634 844411 (F) 0634 830991
LAWTEC	4th Floor Duchy House 96 Lancaster Road Preston PR1 1HE	(T) 0772 200035 (F) 0772 54801

TEC Name	Address	Tel & Fax No
Leeds TEC	Belgrave Hall Belgrave Street Leeds LS2 8DD	(T) 0532 347666 (F) 0532 438126
Leicestershire TEC	Meridian East Meridian Business Centre Leicester LE3 2WZ	(T) 0533 651515 (F) 0533 515226
Lincolnshire TEC	5th Floor Wigford House Brayford Wharf East Lincoln LN5 7AY	(T) 0522 532266 (F) 0522 510534
London East TEC	Cityside House 40 Adler Street London E1 1EE	(T) 071 377 1866 (F) 071 377 8003
Manchester TEC	Bouton House 17–21 Chorlton Street Manchester M1 3HY	(T) 061 236 7222 (F) 061 236 8878
Merseyside TEC	3rd Floor Tithebarn House Tithebarn Street Liverpool L2 2NZ	(T) 051 236 0026 (F) 051 236 4013
METROTEC	Buckingham Row Northway Wigan WN1 1XX	(T) 0942 36312 (F) 0942 821410

TEC Name	Address	Tel & Fax No
Mid Glamorgan TEC	Unit 17–20 Centre Court Main Avenue	(T) 0443 841594
	Treforest Industrial Estate Pontypridd Mid Glamorgan CF37 5YL	(F) 0443 841578
Milton Keynes & North Buckinghamshire TEC	Old Market Halls Creed Street	(T) 0908 222555
	Wolverton Milton Keynes MK12 5LY	(F) 0908 222839
Norfolk & Waveney TEC	Partnership House Unit 10	(T) 0603 763812
	Norwich Business Park Whiting Road Norwich NR4 6DJ	(F) 0603 763813
NORMIDTEC	Spencer House Dewhurst Road	(T) 0925 826515
	Birchwood Warrington WA3 7PP	(F) 0603 763813
North Derbyshire TEC	Block C St Marys Court	(T) 0246 551158
	St Marys Gate Chesterfield S41 7TD	(F) 0246 238489
North East Wales TEC	Wynnstay Block Hightown Barracks	(T) 0978 290049
	Kingsmill Road Wrexham Clwyd LL13 8BH	(F) 0978 290061

TEC Name	Address	Tel & Fax No
North London TEC	Dumayne House 1 Fox Lane Palmers Green London N13 4AB	(T) 081 447 9422 (F) 081 882 5931
North Nottinghamshire TEC	1st Floor Block C Edwinstowe House High Street Edwinstowe Mansfield Nottinghamshire NG21 9PR	(T) 0623 824624 (F) 0623 824070
North West London TEC	Kirkfield House 118–120 Station Road Harrow Middlesex HA1 2RL	(T) 081 424 8866 (F) 081 424 2240
North Yorkshire TEC	TEC House 7 Pioneer Business Park Amy Johnson Way Clifton Moorgate York YO3 8TN	(T) 0904 691939 (F) 0904 690411
Northamptonshire TEC	Royal Pavilion Summerhouse Pavilion Summerhouse Road Moulton Park Northampton NN3 1WD	(T) 0604 671200 (F) 0604 670361
Northumberland TEC	Suite 2 Craster Court Manor Walk Shopping Centre Cramlington NE23 6XX	(T) 0670 713303 (F) 0670 713323

TEC Name	Address	Tel & Fax No
Oldham TEC	Meridian Centre King Street Oldham OL8 1EZ	(T) 061 620 0006 (F) 061 620 0030
Powys TEC	1st Floor St David's House Newtown Powys SY16 1RB	(T) 0686 622494 (F) 0686 622716
QUALITEC (St Helens) Ltd	7 Waterside Court Technology Campus St Helens Merseyside WA9 1UE	(T) 0744 24433 (F) 0744 453030
Rochdale TEC	St James Place 160–162 Yorkshire Street Rochdale Lancashire OL16 2DL	(T) 0706 44909 (F) 0706 49979
Rotherham TEC	Moorgate House Moorgate Road Rotherham S60 2EN	(T) 0709 830511 (F) 0709 362519
Sandwell TEC	1st Floor Kingston House 438–450 High Street West Bromwich West Midlands B70 9LD	(T) 021 525 4242 (F) 021 525 4250
Sheffield TEC	St Mary's Court 55 St Mary's Road Sheffield S2 4AQ	(T) 0742 701911 (F) 0742 752634

TEC Name	Address	Tel & Fax No
Shropshire TEC	2nd Floor 55 St Mary's Court St Mary's Road Sheffield S2 4AQ	(T) 0952 291471 (F) 0952 291437
SOLOTEC	Lancaster House 7 Elmfield Road Bromley Kent BR1 1LT	(T) 081 313 9232 (F) 081 313 2945
Somerset TEC	Crescent House 3–7 The Mount Taunton Somerset TA1 3TT	(T) 0823 259121 (F) 0823 256174
South & East Cheshire TEC	PO Box 37 Middlewich Industrial Park Dalton Way Middlewich Cheshire CW10 0HU	(T) 0606 737009 (F) 0606 737022
South Glamorgan TEC	3–7 Drakes Walk Waterfront 2000 Atlantic Wharf Cardiff CF1 5AN	(T) 0222 451000 (F) 0222 450424
South Thames TEC	200 Great Dover Street London SE1 4YB	(T) 071 403 1990 (F) 071 378 1590
Southern Derbyshire TEC	St Helens Court St Helens Street Derby DE1 3GY	(T) 0332 290550 (F) 0332 292188

TEC Name	Address	Tel & Fax No
Staffordshire TEC	Festival Way Festival Park Stoke on Trent Staffordshire ST1 5TQ	(T) 0782 202733 (F) 0782 286215
Stockport/High Peak TEC	1 St Peters Square Stockport SK1 1NN	(T) 061 477 8830 (F) 061 480 7243
Suffolk TEC	2nd Floor Crown House Crown Street Ipswich IP1 3HS	(T) 0473 218951 (F) 0473 231776
Surrey TEC	Technology House 48–54 Goldsworth Road Woking Surrey GU21 1LE	(T) 0483 728190 (F) 0483 755259
Sussex TEC	2nd Floor Electrowatt House North Street Horsham West Sussex RH12 1RS	(T) 0403 271471 (F) 0403 272082
TARGED TEC	Llys Brittania Parc Menai Bangor Gwynedd LL57 4BN	(T) 0248 671444 (F) 0248 670889
Teesside TEC	Training & Enterprise House 2 Queens Square Middlesborough Cleveland TS2 1AA	(T) 0642 231023 (F) 0642 232480

TEC Name	Address	Tel & Fax No
Thames Valley Enterprise	6th Floor Kings Point 120 Kings Road Reading RG1 3BZ	(T) 0734 568156 (F) 0734 567908
Tyneside TEC	Moongate House 5th Avenue Business Park Team Valley Trading Estate Gateshead NE11 OHF	(T) 091 487 5599 (F) 091 482 6519
Wakefield TEC	Grove Hall 60 College Grove Road Wakefield WF1 3RN	(T) 0924 299907 (F) 0924 201837
Walsall TEC	5th Floor Townend House Townend Square Walsall WS1 1NS	(T) 0922 32332 (F) 0922 33011
Wearside TEC	Derwent House New Town Centre Washington Tyne and Wear NE38 7ST	(T) 091 416 6161 (F) 091 415 1093
West London TEC	Sovereign Court 15–21 Staines Road Hounslow Middlesex TW3 3HA	(T) 081 577 1010 (F) 081 570 9969
West Wales TEC	Orchard House Orchard Street Swansea West Glamorgan SA1 5DJ	(T) 0792 460355 (F) 0792 456341

TEC Name	Address	Tel & Fax No
Wight Training & Enterprise	Mill Court Furrlongs Newport Isle of Wight PO30 2AA	(T) 0983 822818 (F) 0983 527063
Wiltshire TEC	The Bora Buildings Westlea Campus Westlea Downs Swindon Wiltshire SN5 7EZ	(T) 0793 513644 (F) 0793 542006
Wolverhampton TEC	Pendeford Business Park Wobaston Road Wolverhampton WV9 5HA	(T) 0902 397787 (F) 0902 397786

Awarding Bodies – List of Abbreviations

Awarding Body (abbrev)	Full Title	Address
AAT	Association of Accounting Technicians	154 Clerkenwell Road London EC1R 5AD (T) 071 837 8600 (F) 071 837 6970
ABPI	The Association of the British Pharmaceutical Industry	12 Whitehall London SW1A 2DY (T) 071 930 3477 (F) 071 930 3290
ABTA–NTB	Association of British Travel Agents National Training Board	Waterloo House 11–17 Chertsey Road Woking Surrey GU21 5AL (T) 0483 727321 (F) 0483 756698
ACILB	Animal Care Industry Lead Body Shelters	c/o Wood Green Animal London Road Godmanchester Huntingdon PE18 8LJ (T) 0480 831177 (F) 0480 830566
ACTD	Association for Ceramic Tiling Development	2nd Floor Federation House Station Road Stoke on Trent ST4 2SA (T) 0782 745335 (F) 0782 745336

Awarding Body (abbrev)	Full Title	Address
ATA	Aviation Training Association	125 London Road High Wycombe HP11 1BT (T) 0494 445262 (F) 0494 439984
BAGMA	British Agricultural and Garden Machinery Association Ltd	Church Street Rickmansworth Herts WD3 1RQ (T) 0923 720241
BCS	The British Computer Society	PO Box 1454 Station Road Swindon SN1 1TG (T) 0793 480269
BCTLTD	Bus and Coach Training Ltd	Gable House 40 High Street Rickmansworth WD3 1ER (T) 0923 896607 (F) 0923 896881
BFM	British Furniture Manufacturers Federation	30 Harcourt Street London W1H 2AA (T) 071 724 0854
BFMF	British Footwear Manufacturers Federation	Royalty House 72 Dean Street London W1V 5HB (T) 071 734 0951
BFPA	British Fibreboard Packaging Association	2 Saxon Court Freeschool Street Northampton NN1 4HL (T) 0604 21002 (F) 0604 20636
BG	British Gas Plc	100 Rochester Row London SW1P 1JB (T) 071 821 1444 (F) 071 828 1442

AWARDING BODIES – LIST OF ABBREVIATIONS

Awarding Body (abbrev)	Full Title	Address
BHS	The British Horse Society	British Equestrian Centre Stoneleigh Kenilworth Warwickshire CV8 2LR (T) 0203 696697
BICS	British Institute of Cleaning Science	Whitworth Chambers George Row Northampton NN1 1DF (T) 0604 230075
BII	British Institute of Innkeeping	51/53 High Street Camberley Surrey GU15 3RG (T) 0276 684449
BPICS	British Production and Inventory Control Society	University of Warwick Science Park Sir William Lyons Road Coventry CV4 7EZ (T) 0203 692266 (F) 0203 692305
BPTA	British Polymer Training Association	Coppice House Halesfield 7 Telford Shropshire TF4 4NA (T) 0952 587020 (F) 0952 582065
BPTC	Building Products Training Council	c/o British Ceramics Confederation Station Road Stoke on Trent ST4 2SA (T) 0782 744631 (F) 0782 744102
BSA	British Sign Association	Swan House 297 Balham High Road London SW17 7BQ

Awarding Body (abbrev)	Full Title	Address
BTEC	Business and Technology Education Council	Central House Upper Woburn Place London WC1H 0HH (T) 071 413 8400 (F) 071 387 6068
C&G	City and Guilds of London Institute	46 Britannia Street London WC1X 9RG (T) 071 278 2468 (F) 071 278 9460
CABWI	The Certification and Assessment Board for the Water Industry	1 Queen Anne's Gate London SW1H 9BT (T) 071 957 4523 (F) 071 957 4641
CCBCITB	China Clay & Ball Clay Industries Training Board	John Keay House St Austell Cornwall PL25 4DJ (T) 0726 74482
CCETSW	Central Council for Education and Training in Social Work	Derbyshire House St Chad's Street London WC1 8AD
CEYA	Council for Early Years Awards	26/28 Binney Street London W1Y 1YN (T) 071 629 0516 (F) 071 409 7961
CIA	Chemical Industries Association	Kings Buildings Smith Square London SW1P 3JJ (T) 071 834 3399 (F) 071 834 4469
CIB	The Chartered Institute of Bankers	10 Lombard Street London EC3V 9AS (T) 071 623 3531 (F) 071 283 1510

AWARDING BODIES — LIST OF ABBREVIATIONS

Awarding Body (abbrev)	Full Title	Address
CIBTAC	Confederation of International Beauty Therapy and Cosmetology	2nd Floor 34 Imperial Square Cheltenham GL50 1QZ (T) 0242 570284
CII	The Chartered Insurance Institute	20 Aldermanbury London EC2V 7HY (T) 071 606 3835 (F) 071 726 0131
CIOB	The Chartered Institute of Building	Englemere Kings Rise Ascot Berks SL5 8BJ (T) 0344 23355
CITB	Construction Industry Training Board	Bircham Newton Near Kings Lynn PE31 6RH (T) 0553 776677 (F) 0553 692226
CITBNI	Construction Industry Training Board Northern Ireland	17 Dundrod Road Crumlin BT29 4SR (T) 0232 825466
DTF	The Dairy Trade Federation Ltd	19 Cornwall Terrace London NW1 4QP (T) 071 486 7244 (F) 071 487 4734
ECITB	Engineering Construction Industry Training Board	Blue Court Church Lane Kings Langley Herts (T) 0923 260000
EnTra	Engineering Training Authority	41 Clarendon Road Watford Herts WD1 1HS (T) 0923 238441 (F) 0923 256086

231

Awarding Body (abbrev)	Full Title	Address
EOSM	The Electronics Office Systems Maintenance Lead Body	c/o The Electronics Exam Board Savoy Hill House Savoy Hill London WC2R 0BS (T) 071 836 3357
ETA	Electricity Training Association	30 Millbank London SW1P 4RD (T) 071 344 5700 (F) 071 233 6640
ETCNI	Electricity Training Council (Northern Ireland)	The Design Centre 39 Corporation Street Belfast BT1 3RA (T) 0232 329878 (F) 0232 310301
FASTCO	Forestry and Arboriculture Safety and Training Council	231 Corstorphine Road Edinburgh EH12 7AT (T) 031 334 8083 (F) 031 334 3047
FCRA Ltd	Fabric Care Research Association Ltd	Forest House Laboratories Knaresborough Road Harrogate HG2 7LZ (T) 0423 885977
FDQC	Food and Drink Qualifications Council	c/o Dairy Foundation 19 Cornwall Terrace London NW1 4PQ (T) 071 486 7244
GCL	The Guild of Cleaners and Launderers	73 Fosseway Landsdowne Park Clevedon Avon BS21 5ET (T) 0275 342328

Awarding Body (abbrev)	Full Title	Address
GTL	Glass Training Limited	BGMC Building Northumberland Road Sheffield S10 2UA (T) 0742 661494 (T) 0742 669263 (F) 0742 660738
HCIMA	Hotel, Catering and Institutional Management Association	191 Trinity Road London SW17 7HN (T) 081 672 4251
HCTC	Hotel and Catering Training Company	High Street, Ealing London W5 5DB (T) 081 579 2400 (F) 081 840 6217
HMC	Henley Management College	Greenlands Henley on Thames RG9 3AU (T) 0491 571454 (F) 0491 571635
HTB	Hairdressing Training Board	3 Chequer Road Doncaster DN1 2AA (T) 0302 342837 (F) 0302 323381
HVDE	Heating Ventilating and Domestic Engineering National Joint Industry Council	ESCA House 34 Palace Road Bayswater London W2 4JG (T) 071 229 2488 (F) 071 727 9268
IITC	Insurance Industry Training Council	271a High Street Orpington Kent BR6 0NW (T) 0689 896711 (F) 0689 896905

Awarding Body (abbrev)	Full Title	Address
ILBAH	Industry Lead Body for Amenity Horticulture	c/o Local Government Management Board Arndale House Arndale Centre Luton LU1 2YS (T) 0582 451166
IM	The Institute of Management	Management House Cottingham Road Corby Northants NN17 1TT (T) 0536 204222 (F) 0536 201651
IMBM	The Institute of Maintenance and Building Management	Keets House 30 East Street Farnham Surrey GU9 7SW (T) 0252 710994
IMEAT	Institute of Meat	Langford Bristol BS18 7DY (T) 0934 853018 (F) 0934 852741
IMI	The Institute of the Motor Industry	Fanshaws Brickendon Hertford SG13 8PQ (T) 0992 511521
IOH	The Institute of Housing	Octavia House Westwood Business Park Westwood Way Coventry CV4 8JP (T) 0203 694433
ISM	Institute of Supervisory Management	Mansell House 22 Bore Street Lichfield Staffs WS13 6LP (T) 0543 251346

Awarding Body (abbrev)	Full Title	Address
ITD	The Institute of Training and Development	Institute Road Marlow Bucks SL7 1BN (T) 0628 890123 (F) 0628 890208
ITITO	Information Technology Industry Training Organisation	16 South Molton Street London W1Y 1DE (T) 071 355 4924
JAB	Joint Awarding Bodies (C&G, CCETSW)	Contact as for C&G. BTEC is awarding these qualifications separately
JCFHG	Joint Council for Fish Husbandry and Gamekeeping	Valley Farm Stoke Andover ST11 0NR (T) 0264 738318
JIBPMES	The Joint Industry Board for Plumbing Mechanical Engineering Services in England and Wales	Brook House Brook Street St Neots Huntingdon Cambs PE19 2HW (T) 0480 476925 (F) 0480 403081
JNHETC	Joint National Horse Education and Training Council	The Stables Rossington Hall Great North Road Doncaster DN11 0HN (T) 0302 864242
LCCI	The London Chamber of Commerce and Industry Examinations Board	Marlowe House Station Road Sidcup Kent DA15 7BJ (T) 081 302 0261 (F) 081 302 4169

Awarding Body (abbrev)	Full Title	Address
LGMB	Local Government Management Board	Arndale House Arndale Centre Luton Beds LU1 2TS (T) 0582 451166
LITO	Leathergoods Industry Training Organisation	Walsall Chamber of Commerce & Industry Wednesbury Training Centre St Pauls Road Wood Green Wednesbury West Midlands WS10 9QX (T) 021 556 0959
M&ETA	Marine and Engineering Training Association	30–38 Cambridge Street Aylesbury Bucks HP20 1RS (T) 0296 434943 (F) 0296 437124
MCI*	Management Charter Initiative	Russell Square House 10–12 Russell Square London WC1B 5BZ (T) 071 872 9000 (F) 071 872 9099
MITSC	Motor Industry Training Standards Council	201 Great Portland Street London W1N 6AB (T) 071 436 6373
MMFITAB	Man-Made Fibres Industry Training Advisory Board	Central House Gate Lane Sutton Coldfield B73 5TS (T) 021 355 7022

* MCI is a joint awarding body. It does not make its own awards, but works with other awarding bodies offering NVQs based on the National Standards for managers and supervisors.

Awarding Body (abbrev)	Full Title	Address
MVC	Management Verification Consortium Ltd	344–354 Gray's Inn Road London WC1X 8BP (T) 071 278 4411
NAPHMSC	National Association of Plumbing, Heating and Mechanical Services Contractors	Ensign House Ensign Business Centre Westwood Way Coventry CV4 8JA (T) 0203 470626 (F) 0203 470942
NEA	Neighbourhood Energy Action	2–4 Bigg Market Newcastle upon Tyne NE1 1UW
NEBAHAI	National Examinations Board for Agriculture, Horticulture & Allied Industries	46 Britannia Street London WC1X 1UW (T) 071 278 2468 (F) 071 278 9640
NEBSM	The National Examining Board for Supervisory Management	76 Portland Place London W1N 4AA (T) 071 278 2468
NPTC	National Proficiency Tests Council for Agriculture and Horticulture	National Agricultural Centre Tenth Street Stoneleigh Kenilworth CV8 2LG (T) 0203 696553
NQC	Newspaper Qualifications Council	The Newspaper Society Bloomsbury House Bloomsbury Square 74–77 Great Russell Street London WC1B 3DA (T) 071 636 7014 (F) 071 631 5119

Awarding Body (abbrev)	Full Title	Address
NRTC	National Retail Training Council	4th Floor Bedford House 69–79 Fulham High Street London SW6 3JW (T) 071 371 5021 (F) 071 371 9160
NTTG	National Textiles Training Group	c/o Knitting & Lace Industries Training Resource Agency 7 Gregory Boulevard Nottingham NG7 6LD (T) 0602 605330 (F) 0602 625450
NWTC	National Wholesale Training Council	I-Mex House 40 Princess Street Manchester M1 6DE (T) 061 237 9199
PA	Paintmakers Association of Great Britain	Alembic House 93 Albert Embankment London SE1 7TY (T) 071 582 1185 (F) 071 735 0616
OU	The Open University Validation Services	344–354 Gray's Inn Road London WC1X 8BP (T) 071 278 4411
PEI	Pitman Examinations Institute	Catteshall Manor Godalming Surrey GU7 1UU (T) 0483 415311 (F) 0483 423994 (F) 0483 860435
PESC	Petroleum Employers' Skills Council	Suite 1, 314–322 Regent Street London W1R 4AB (T) 071 255 2335

Awarding Body (abbrev)	Full Title	Address
PMI	The Pensions Management Institute	PMI House 4–10 Artillery Lane London E1 7LS (T) 071 247 1452 (F) 071 375 0603
PQB	Publishing Qualifications Board	Book House 45 East Hill Wandsworth London SW18 2QZ (T) 081 871 1989
PSLB	Purchasing and Supply Lead Body	Institute of Purchasing and Supply Easton House Easton on the Hill Stamford Lincs PE9 3NZ (T) 0780 56777
PTC	Periodicals Training Council	Imperial House 15–19 Kingsway London WC2B 6UN (T) 071 836 8798
QFI	Qualifications for Industry Ltd	80 Richardshaw Lane Pudsey Leeds LS28 6BN (T) 0532 393355 (F) 0532 393155
QPTC	Quarry Products Training Council	Sterling House Station Road Gerrards Cross Bucks SL9 8HT (T) 0753 891808 (F) 0753 891132

Awarding Body (abbrev)	Full Title	Address
RCPAITC	Refractories, Clay Pipes & Allied Industries Training Council	c/o University of Sheffield School of Materials Elmfield Northumberland Road Sheffield S10 2TZ (T) 0742 768555 x6093
REATEA	The Residential Estate Agency Training and Education Association	The Avenue Brampford Speke Exeter EX5 5DW (T) 0392 841194
RSA	RSA Examinations Board	Progress House Westwood Way Coventry CV4 8HS (T) 0203 470033 (F) 0203 468080
RTBTB	Racing and Thoroughbred Breeding Training Board	The Stables Rossington Hall Great North Road Doncaster DN11 0HN (T) 0302 864242
RTITBS	RTITB Services Ltd	National Vocational Assessment MOTEC Telford High Ercall Telford TF6 6RB (T) 0952 770441
SAMSA	Silica and Moulding Sands Association	Quartz House 18 Warwick Street Rugby CV21 3DH (T) 0788 573041 (F) 0788 560316
SFIA	Sea Fish Industry Authority	Seafish House St Andrews Dock Hull HU3 4QE (T) 0482 27837 (F) 0482 223310

AWARDING BODIES — LIST OF ABBREVIATIONS

Awarding Body (abbrev)	Full Title	Address
SITO	Security Industry Training Organisation	Security House Barbourne Road Worcester WR1 1RS (T) 0905 20004 (F) 0905 613625
SIQB	Steel Industry Board	PO Box 32 Sheffield Road Rotherham S60 1AG (T) 0709 371234 x5572
SPA(UK)LTD	Screen Printing Association (UK) Ltd	Association House 7a West Street Reigate Surrey RH2 9BL (T) 0737 240792
SRITO	Shoe Repair Industry Training Organisation	76 The Parade Sutton Coldfield West Midlands B72 1PD (T) 021 355 2033
TTF	Timber Trade Federation Ltd	Clarville House 26 Oxendon Street London SW17 4EL (T) 071 839 1891
TITO	Tobacco Industry Training Organisation	Glen House Stag Place London SW1E 5AG (T) 071 828 2803 (F) 071 630 2963
TVSC	Telecommunications Vocational Standards Council	1st Floor Dacom House Presley Way Crownhill Milton Keynes MK8 0HD (T) 0908 265500 (F) 0908 262285

Awarding Body (abbrev)	Full Title	Address
UODLE	University of Oxford Delegacy of Local Examinations	Ewert House Ewert Place Summertown Oxford OX2 7BZ (T) 0865 515638
VTCT	Vocational Training Charitable Trust	46 Aldwick Road Bognor Regis West Sussex PO21 2PN (T) 0243 842064 (F) 0243 821299
WAMITAB	Waste Management Industry Training and Advisory Board	9 Saxon Court St Peters Gardens Northampton NN1 1SX (T) 0604 20426

Glossary of Terms

Accreditation Formal recognition that individuals have shown evidence of performance which meets specified standards.

Assessment (competence-based) Collection of evidence of performance by a variety of methods.

Awards A general term for qualifications issued by examining or validating bodies, ie certificates, diplomas etc.

Awarding body An examining or validating body. In a competence-based system, an awarding body has central responsibility for the quality, but not the methods of assessment.

Competence The ability to perform a particular activity to a prescribed standard. Competence is a wide concept which embodies the ability to transfer skills and knowledge to new situations within the occupational area. It encompasses organisation and planning of work, innovation and coping with non-routine activities. It includes those qualities of personal effectiveness that are required in the workplace to deal with co-workers, managers and customers.

Continuous assessment Assessment of competence on every occasion it is required during normal workplace activity. Used for formative assessment and to arrive at a cumulative judgement for final assessment purposes.

Credit accumulation A system by which individuals can accumulate units of competence. When a specified combination of units has been achieved the individual can obtain a full NVQ.

Credit transfer The use of an award (or credits towards one) as credit towards another award.

Element of competence The descriptors of the activities necessary for the completion of the function described in a unit of competence.

Formative assessment Assessment during a course, or over a period of workplace activity which collects evidence of performance.

Industry Lead Body An organisation comprised of industry education and trades union representatives with formal responsibility for the development of national standards of occupational competence and a framework of National Vocational Qualifications.

Moderation A process or procedure to align standards of assessment between different test papers, different testing occasions, different examiners, different centres etc.

National Vocational Qualification A statement of competence defined by industry and based on nationally agreed standards of occupational competence.

Norm-referenced assessment Assessment of an individual's ability in order to determine how well it compares with other individuals' abilities.

Occupational Standards Council (OSC) A group of Industry Lead Bodies responsible for management of cross-industry standards and NVQs.

Performance criteria Descriptors of required outcomes of workplace activities.

Range statements Descriptors of the limits within which performance to the identified standard is expected if an individual is to be deemed competent. Range describes competent workplace performance, not the situations in which performance must be observed for assessment purposes.

Unit of competence A descriptor of a discrete function carried out by an individual within an occupational area.

Underpinning skills and knowledge Identifies the knowledge and skill necessary to perform to the standards identified by the performance criteria in the contexts identified in the range statement.

Who to Contact

What NVQs are available?	Regular NCVQ update *Monitor* from NCVQs 222 Euston Road London NW1 2BZ
What standards are available?	Relevant Industry Lead body (ILB) (see list on p 179)
What standards are under development (if no ILB)?	Training Enterprise and Education Directorate (TEED) Qualifications and Standards Branch Room E454 Moorfoot Sheffield S1 4PQ *Standards Digest* available from TEED (above) Relevant awarding body (see list on p 227)
How do you get access to the NCVQ database?	NCVQ 222 Euston Road London NW1 2BZ

What NVQs are available?	NCVQ database (above) or relevant Industry Lead Body
How do you get in-company training recognised for credit exemption/advanced standing?	your local college/poly
What about qualifications in Scotland (SVQs)?	Scotvec Hanover House Douglas St Glasgow G2 7NQ

Funding support – what is available?

As more NVQs are developed and the implementation increases, so levels and types of funding available to support implementation are generated.

The main source of information regarding funding should be your local Training and Enterprise Council (TEC) (LECs in Scotland). A full list of addresses and telephone numbers is included in Part III.

Help is available under a number of headings, these include:

Investors in People
Business Change
Business Development
Competence Audits/NVQ Service
Skill Choice
Training Credits
Gateways to Learning
Training for Work.

Further information on the Skill Choice initiative is provided on page 99. This will probably be the best source of funding in respect of NVQ implementation for employers, providing a percentage of costs in respect of action planning (guidance), assessment planning and accreditation.

For Investors in People the TECs provide approved consultants to help with action planning and to undertake the assessment (see p 76).

Business Change provides support with actions for change within the organisation.

TECs hold registers of approved consultants and providers. There is a regional and national register known as TECAssure. This will include the names of all approved individual consultants (they have to pay a fee for the approval process).

Some TECs also pay full fees for one of their approved consultants to undertake a 'competence audit' and 'action plan' – this will produce a detailed plan with costings for the introduction of NVQs in the most cost-effective and productive way. This is a worthwhile service which can save a great deal of time and money in the long-run.

For further information, see the sections in this publication on 'What are TECs....', 'Skill Choice', 'Investors in People' and 'Assessor and Verifier Awards'. Then contact your local TEC and see what is available.

References

BTEC (1990) *APL: General Guidelines* Business and Technician Education Council: London.

CGLI (1988) *Assessment and Validation Procedures for APL* City and Guilds: London.

C&G (1990) *Guidelines on Accreditation of Prior Learning* City and Guilds: London.

CNAA (1984) *Access to Higher Education. Non-standards entry to CNAA first degree and Dip HE courses* Council for National Academic Awards: London.

Coopers and Lybrand (1985) *A Challenge to Complacency; Changing Attitudes to Training* Manpower Services Commission/National Economic Development Commission: Sheffield.

Employment Dept (1993) *TECS 1992*

Employment Dept (1990) *Training and Enterprise Councils; A Prospectus for the 1990s*

Employment Dept (1991) *Development of Assessable Standards for National Certification* Standards/Methodology Unit (edited by Edward Fennell) HMSO: London (new guidelines expected in 1995)

Fletcher, S, (1993) *Quality and Competence,* Kogan Page: London

Fletcher, S, (1992a) *Designing Competence Based Training,* Kogan Page: London

Fletcher, S, (1992b) *Competence based Assessment Techniques* Kogan Page: London

HMSO (1986) *Working Together, Education and Training* Government White Paper Cmnd 9823, Department of Employment, HMSO: London.

Mansfield, B and Mathews, D (1985) *Job Competence: A Description for Use in Vocational Education and Training* FESC/ESF Core Skills Project: Bristol.

MSC (1981) *A New Training Initiative: Agenda for Action* Manpower Services Commission: Sheffield.

MSC/NEDC (1986) *Review of Vocational Qualifications in England and Wales*

NCVQ (1988a) *The NVQ Criteria and Related Guidance* NCVQ: London.

NCVQ (1988b) *NVQs – What They Mean for You – A Guide*

NCVQ (1988c) *Draft Corporate Plan 1988/9 – 1991/2* NCVQ: London.

NCVQ (1989) 'Occupational standards for dental surgery assistants', *NCVQ R&D Report*, 1, December

NCVQ (quarterly) *NVQ Monitor*, NCVQ: London.

NCVQ (1993) *The Common Accord* Employment Department: Sheffield.

NEDC/MSC (1984) *Competence and Competition: Training and Education in the Federal Republic of Germany, The United States and Japan* National Economic Development Office and Manpower Services Commission: Sheffield.

Randell, G (1984) *Staff Appraisal*, 3rd Ed, Institute of Personnel Management: London.

Scotvec (1988) *The National Certificate. A Guide to Assessment* Scotvec: Glasgow.

Training Agency (1988/90) *Competence and Assessment* Standards Methodology Unit, Moorfoot, Sheffield.

Training Agency (1989) *Training and Enterprise, Priorities for Action 1990/91*

Index